WHY I STOPPED LISTENING TO RUSH

Confessions of a Recovering Neocon

DAVID ALAN BLACK

PublishAmerica
Baltimore

First printing

ISBN: 1-4137-3019-1
PUBLISHED BY PUBLISHAMERICA, LLLP
www.publishamerica.com
Baltimore

Printed in the United States of America

To my wife

TABLE OF CONTENTS

— Preface —

While I write these words, my wife and I are completing the construction of our new house on our Virginia farm. Naked wires dangle where light fixtures will soon burn brightly, and freshly laid floorboards will soon be covered with stain and varnish. If you've ever gone through this process, you don't need any further explanation. The one thing that keeps us going is the knowledge that one day the house will be finished!

Building a nation is a lot like building a house. And, as you well know, there are hundreds of blueprints out there, each vying for our attention. As I've thought about this great country of ours, I've discovered that certain principles don't change. God's original blueprint for America is still available. Admittedly, like building a new house, the process can be lengthy, costly, messy, and hard work. But it's not impossible. In fact, when you consider the alternative, it's well worth the time and effort involved.

The following "building plans" are presented to America's sons and daughters so that they may be sturdy citizens of the Red, White, and Blue, and especially good soldiers of the Old Rugged Cross. I trust these chapters will be helpful to you.

— *Chapter 1* —

Introduction: Not So Much a Book
as a Way of Thinking

This book is about common sense and hope. While it addresses social and political issues, it is first and foremost a book about the practical issues we all deal with on a daily basis. It is a book about the dramatic changes taking place in our society and the signs of a visible shift of thinking away from our nation's biblical and constitutional foundations. Above all it is a call for Americans to return to the personal values and beliefs that have sustained our great nation throughout its history. For those of us who would like to have an impact on our culture, and to those for whom religious freedom means more than the right to preach a simplistic and one-dimensional gospel, this book may perhaps serve as a statement of purpose.

With the election of George W. Bush and the tragedy of September 11, 2001, there arose a new vision of America. America would now use its military power to reshape world politics, crush tyrannical regimes, and establish "democracies" in their place. On the domestic front, there would no longer be any question of reducing the size of the federal government. The only question now was whether government growth would be merely big or gigantic.

When traditional conservatives like myself voted for Bush in 2000, we had no idea that this policy agenda would be in effect just two years into the Bush administration. Many of us who had lived abroad had a growing concern about the anti-American feeling around the world. It was therefore with delight that we heard candidate Bush speak of a "humbler" foreign policy and of reducing U.S. forces overseas. We also anticipated that the new administration would embrace conservative objectives such as tax cuts, smaller government, fiscal responsibility, a balanced budget, protection of individual rights, and support for state and local governments.

None of this has happened. Instead, a constitutional *coup d'etat* has occurred. Today the fundamental beliefs of our Founding Fathers are being subverted as never before. In the name of an all-powerful state, our precious God-given freedoms are being stripped away, one freedom at a time. Our political, media, and educational establishments are now controlled by people who pay as much attention to the Constitution as you and I do to our junk e-mail. Statism on the right has become indistinguishable from statism on the left. Most disturbing of all, few Americans seem concerned about losing their freedoms. After all, we can trust our government, can't we?

There are times in life when anyone with a shred of principle should be profoundly angry. I believe this is such a time in our nation's history. It is a lie and a deception to pretend that Bush's religious convictions justify his unbiblical and unconstitutional vision of government. I am convinced that the time has come to secede from "compassionate conservatism." I've had all I can take of George W. Bush and his officious strutting, of exaggerated intelligence reports "justifying" attacks on sovereign nations, of the distortion of facts and reliance on rumor to influence public opinion, and of Rumsfeld & Co. hiding behind a curtain of PR spin while sending hundreds of brave Americans to their deaths in Afghanistan and Iraq. I'm outraged by our self-serving promotion of "democracy" and our support of petty dictators and monarchs (as long as they continue to provide us with a steady stream of Middle Eastern oil, that is). I'm tired of duplicity, doublespeak, "embedded" journalists, contradictions in our foreign policy, Washington's control over the media, and judicial activism run amok.

Just as troubling to me is the fact that the church in America has accepted the myth of neutrality. Never have evangelical Christians tried to be so "relevant." Never have they been so irrelevant. Most theologians and pastors have even gone so far as to cultivate a careful silence on the real issues facing America today. For all intents and purposes, God has become an adjunct of man, a help in the work of the church and in procuring victory in our man-made wars. The Power that humbled Job no longer finds an echo in the American psyche. Ours has become a religion without deeds. Acceptance of the status quo has replaced principle. Where, I ask, are the Christian men and women who will stand up and fight in the political arena without compromise? They are scarcely to be found.

Recently I received this letter at my website, daveblackonline.com:

Mr. Black:

Prayer and Bible reading was not taken away in 1962 and 1963 by the government or the judges. It was *given up* by the churches and Christians.

Abortion on demand was not forced on America in 1973, it was *allowed* by the churches and Christians.

It is that same do-nothing, apathetic, cowardice attitude that has permeated our churches and the minds of Christians that will cause millions, who should support [former Alabama Supreme Court Chief Justice] Judge Moore, to tuck their tail and run and hide behind their Republican house of cards that is built on sinking sand.

It's a sad state of affairs when professing Christians have to "step out of character" to support righteousness.

Judge Moore is standing for righteousness. Those who don't stand with him…well, enough said.

Whatever King Bush says they will support. The commandment to have no other gods before Him seems to have been ignored by a most unlikely group of folks.

I'm afraid we have reached, in America, what is described in the second half of Proverbs, chapter 1. Our calamity is coming, and soon.

Tragically, the author of this letter is absolutely correct. Instead of being committed to a robust defense of the truth, we evangelicals have become evangelifishes who don't have enough time for anyone but ourselves. Instead of exposing evil wherever it is to be found, we delight in criticizing Bill and Hillary and yet are completely blind toward the equally serious transgressions of George W. Bush. Instead of choosing between a secular Caesar and the God of the Old and New Testaments, we gladly endorse big tent politics and its cousin multiculturalism. Instead of engaging our culture, we have succumbed to an excessive preoccupation with the "end times" that has distracted us from acting in the present.

The evidence of our short-sighted acceptance of a post-Christian and post-constitutional philosophy surrounds us everywhere. It's seen in our atrophied brains and addictions to mediocrity. It's seen in our dumbed-down media, our dumbed-down schools, and our dumbed-down churches. It's seen in parents who whine about the public school system yet are too selfish to homeschool their very own flesh and blood. It's seen in the intellectual corruption in the academy and in popular culture.

I am shocked at how many of my very own friends and colleagues clamor for government to take care of them from cradle to grave, completely oblivious to the fact that what Big Brother gives with one hand it always takes away with the other. We should be outraged by our welfare state, our tax burden, our fiat money, our immigration system, our under-supported and over-extended military, our two-party stranglehold, and especially our "compassionate" leaders and their socialist political agenda that has reduced the Constitution to a worthless scrap of paper. The last vestiges of republicanism in America are being destroyed, and that by *conservatives*. Won't anybody stand up to our congressional lawbreakers? Don't we care that our government is raining tyranny down on its people? The promise of the American Revolution was to limit the ability of government to tyrannize the people. So where are the true conservatives who are upholding the rule of law and the Constitution?

I wrote this book because I'm convinced that Rush Limbaugh and his brand of conservatism is the enemy of any citizen who sincerely believes in individual liberty and limited constitutional government. I mention Rush only because he is the leading spokesman of the "Republican Party right or wrong" mentality that pervades conservative talk radio. George W. Bush came into office an advocate of leaner government and then enlarged it by creating a gigantic new cabinet department. He's increased federal spending on a per capita basis more than any other modern president. The pseudo-conservative government in Washington is now the most dangerous power in this country, if not in the world. It is a perfect example of what George Washington once described when he said: "The essence of government is power, and power, lodged as it must be in human hands, will ever be liable to abuse." Indeed, Thomas Jefferson might have been referring to the current administration when he wrote: "The greatest calamity which could befall us would be submission to a government of unlimited power."

Our ruling elites are working feverishly to eradicate all traces of the Constitution in this country. If you don't believe me, read the Constitution and then ask yourself this question: Does any Democrat in government make the slightest attempt to fulfill his oath to "support and defend the Constitution of the United States" or "bear true faith and allegiance to the same"? The same can be asked about practically every Republican as well. For example, both Democrats and Republicans oppose any diversion of money from Social

Security. Both support Social Security taxes. There's only one "minor" problem—Social Security is unconstitutional! Both parties want prescription drug coverage for the elderly, filling a hole in Medicare. The only debate is over how to do it—whether through Medicare itself, or by a private company—and how comprehensive the benefits should be. A plan passed by the Republican-controlled Congress would spend $400 billion to set up a privately administered insurance system. Again, there's a "small" problem. Where does it say in the Constitution that Uncle Sam should use *your* money to pay for *my* prescription drugs?

No doubt about it: our nation is at a crossroads. In order for our country to experience the freedom it once enjoyed, we need a major paradigm shift in our political thinking. The way out of the dilemma is simple. Just reverse the equation. If neither the Democrat Party nor the Republican Party is willing to throw off the shackles of the socialist welfare state, then a third party must do the job, one that will promote constitutional tenets based on certain foundational beliefs about government:

• the belief that our Founding Fathers designed our system of government in the form of a constitutionally limited republic with maximum freedom intended for the people and minimum government control or interference into our personal lives and business affairs.

• the belief that government at all levels was originally intended to be controlled by the people, that the Constitution explicitly restricts the power of the federal government, and that the Bill of Rights guarantees that the government may not infringe on our God-given unalienable rights.

• the belief that power belongs to the states, to local governments, and especially in the hands of "We the People."

• the belief that it's time to end all unconstitutional federal involvement in states issues such as crime, health, education, welfare, and the environment, including social programs such as Social Security and Medicare.

• the belief that all treaties and international agreements not in agreement with the federal government's constitutionally mandated task of protecting the rights of the people should be repealed.

• the belief that the United States should disassociate itself from the United Nations and that the federal government should refrain from meddling in the business and squabbles of foreign nations unless there is an imminent threat to the people of the United States.

Michael Parenti spoke the truth when he said,[1] "The worst forms of tyranny, or certainly the most successful ones, are not those we rail against but those that so insinuate themselves into the imagery of our consciousness, and the fabric of our lives, as not to be perceived as tyranny." When the thirteen colonies came together in 1787 they created the federal government as their agent—not the other way around. It's going to take some brave Americans to send that message to Congress—and some unconventional methods, like saying no to the federal Leviathan that feeds off of both major parties.

This book isn't an anti-conservative polemic per se. It is, however, a sincere and deeply felt statement about the bankruptcy of conservatism in the age in which we live. History has never been open-ended: God always has been and always will be the one who directs it. But our actions are the means God uses, and our choices do make a difference. We cannot say "It's in God's hands" and think we have done our job. We must act, and we must act *now*. If this book encourages even one or two people thinking of ways to staunch the slide of America into totalitarianism, then it will have served its purpose.

— Chapter 2 —

Republic or Empire?
The Rise and Rise of American Power

Many Americans who consider themselves conservatives are actually anti-constitutional neoconservatives. Here's what I mean.

Neocons not only enjoy attacking the left, they fear paleoconservatives and, in particular, all things Southern. Like their arch-hero Lincoln, they believe in an American empire and in unquestioned allegiance to the imperial presidency. The empire they envision cannot tolerate any thought of states rights or regional cultural identity, that is, anything that might question the legitimacy of a central government that snubs its collective nose at traditional cultural values. The proud boast of these neo-imperialists is *Civis Americanus Sum*—and you will become one too, whether you want to or not.

Neocons embrace multiculturalism and therefore support both affirmative action (i.e., reverse racial discrimination) and mass immigration—witness George W. Bush's "compassionate" policy toward *illegal* immigration from Mexico. As for foreign policy, nation building is a big part of their strategy. Paleocons, on the other hand, argue that it is impossible to have a republic as originally envisioned by our Founders and also have an empire at the same time. They are outspoken in their opposition to the invasion and occupation of Iraq because they do not believe you can export democracy at gunpoint. They have this radical notion that the U.S. can hold the torch of liberty high without getting involved in military skirmishes around the globe.

Jimmy Cantrell[2] has done a careful study of the neocons' hang-up over regionalism and especially their love-hate relationship with Southerners. He writes:

> Neocons love the fact that Southerners are naturally opposed to leftist economic claims. They also love the "patriotism" of Southerners as it expresses itself in military service (ditto for English Imperial Conservatives regarding the Scots and Welsh and Irish Protestants). But neocons are fierce to whip Southerners away from recognizing that their Southern cultural affinities and needs are rarely served, and often warred against, by the Imperial USA (ditto for English Imperial Conservatives regarding Scotland, Wales, and even Protestant Northern Ireland, which is nothing but a creation of empire for empire).

This is why paleocons believe that in order to restore the republic, Lincoln must be dethroned—a point convincingly argued by Thomas DiLorenzo, author of the best-selling book *The Real Lincoln*.[3] Paleocons think little of big government with all of its attendant horrors, including an abysmal government "education" system. They feel that the only hope for a rebirth of freedom in America is to get the federal government completely out of every area where it has made such a mess, including health care, education, law enforcement, foreign aid, corporate welfare, and farm subsidies.

Like Congressman Ron Paul of Texas, paleocons want smaller government, an end to the welfare state, and an end to government intrusions into their lives and businesses. They are insulted by a government that says to the country: "You are too immature to care for yourselves, so we in Washington will take care of you."

The paleocon movement has a whiff of revolution about it. Paleocons believe that politicians of both parties have sold out the American people. They want to replace America's arrogant ruling class with citizen legislators. In support of their views, they tend to quote Americans like George Washington, Thomas Jefferson, Patrick Henry, and Stonewall Jackson.

Paleocons don't care much for the bloated, deified federal government. This doesn't make them anarchists. They believe in legitimate authority. What they don't like is having their lives consumed by the state. While neocons love empire, paleocons are quick to point out that all of the great twentieth-century multinational empires have fallen apart. They also note that the Constitution of the United States obligates the federal government to protect the states from foreign invasion, and that our government has failed miserably in this constitutional duty. They ask: If we can send our military halfway around the world to defend the borders of Kuwait and Saudi Arabia, why can't we defend the borders of Arizona, New Mexico, and Texas?

For paleocons, the neocon movement is the legacy of an anti-republican revolution the American people endure only because their elected leaders lack the courage to follow the Constitution, whose defense and implementation should be the first order of business of a free republic. Paleocons realize that men and women will die for freedom, not for some New World Order created for the greedy global mandarins who endlessly lust after power. They argue that only by a return to states rights and responsible local government can America be restored to her former greatness.

One Nation, Under Government?

The root problem of neoconservatism is obvious. It is *hubris*, plain and simple. Neocons feel free to assault the foundational law of the land, and they do so without as much as blinking an eye.

The United States Constitution is unique in its devotion to maximum individual freedom under God's law. Most politicians, on the other hand, believe that social change is the result of politics and state coercion. They believe that society can be radically altered by means of state-financed public education, health education, welfare programs, speech codes, and so on. Christianity, on the other hand, teaches regeneration (John 3:3). Men are not changed by politics but by God.

You would never know this, of course, by listening to President Bush. He consistently ignores our Founders' words that the role of the state is to defend and protect life, liberty, and property. He clearly disregards the teaching of Scripture that the legitimate role of government is to suppress evil and reward the externally obedient by protecting them from the externally disobedient (Romans 13:1-7). Its role is never to make men virtuous. Civil governments that attempt to create a virtuous society are called *totalitarian* governments. Bush's speeches and policy statements, if they do nothing else, prove to every thinking American that the president adheres to the notion of a deified state that can solve all of our nation's problems. His policy agenda is not only unconstitutional but also unbiblical. This includes his so-called faith-based initiative, which may sound inviting but in reality will only make churches dependent on public money, in direct contradiction to Paul's teaching in 1 Corinthians 9:7 that giving is to be completely voluntary. It also ignores a basic New Testament truth: *Jesus had no political agenda.*

Bush, of course, is no Jesus. In fact, he tends to be a social engineer, offering us programs to solve this or that social ill, while Scripture promises a changed life as the result of a personal relationship with God. When the president promises to take care of people's social needs, he directly contradicts the scriptural teaching that men who do not work should not eat. Indeed, the whole idea of a welfare state is based on a violation of the eighth commandment, which prohibits theft. Let's not forget that men like Thomas Jefferson and Patrick Henry protested against a tyrant who was taxing the colonials at a rate of about five percent. Today the average American is taxed at the rate of about 50 percent. Just as importantly, Scripture clearly says it is the church's responsibility to care for the needy in society. God never suggests that this duty should be transferred to the state.

It is all a matter of returning to the foundational document of our nation, the U.S. Constitution. Read it and you will see that it does not promise a perfect society but a free one. The Founders' concept of the state was one that was strictly limited. Their delineation of the role of government may be found in Article 1, Section 8 of the Constitution. Congress is authorized to tax, borrow, and spend to regulate commerce, establish rules for citizenship, establish bankruptcy laws, coin and regulate money, standardize weights and measures, punish counterfeiting, establish a postal service, pass copyright and patent laws, establish federal courts, punish crimes on the high seas, declare war, raise and finance armed forces, establish rules for the armed forces, call up state militias, administer the seat of government, administer federal lands, and pass laws for the implementation of the above. To remove any doubt as to their intentions, the Founders added the Tenth Amendment: "The powers not delegated to the United States...are reserved to the States...or to the people."

This means that there is absolutely no authorization for about 90 percent of what our federal government currently spends. This includes the $14 billion the president has promised for AIDS relief in Africa and the $47 billion our nation spends on Food Stamps annually. There is simply no biblical basis whatsoever for attempting to accomplish Christian objectives through politics, no matter how noble one's intentions may be. Bush's call for taxes, welfare, and state-sponsored health care and education squares neither with the

Bible nor the Constitution, which he took a solemn oath to defend and protect. The solution? Leave the money in the pockets of the taxpayers and let them *voluntarily* give to the charity of their choice. As history shows, that's exactly what they will do.

If you haven't read the Constitution in a while, please go to the Appendix and take a few minutes to ponder its contents. It is an amazingly simple document. It will remind you that the United States was founded on the principles of individual freedom, free markets, private property, and limited government. Once you've read it, you'll find yourself less apt to be seduced into believing that you cannot live without the political paternalism promised by the president.

America's Real Leaders

Thankfully, not everybody has been deceived by the Bush administration's socialist propaganda. At my website, daveblackonline.com, I receive hundreds of e-mails from readers, but few as eloquent as the following one identifying what the author calls America's *real* leaders.

Mr. Black,

I just read your column which quotes Thomas Jackson's correct observation about duty. I can agree with your stance in general, with one exception. You mention our leaders and the biblical command to pray for them. That is indeed a duty we are charged with by our Creator, but let's not pray for the wrong people here.

Elected officials are not our leaders, they are our employees. We are Americans. Americans don't elect leaders. Our leaders come from among us as they did in the 1770s and the 1860s. Bush isn't our boss, he's our butler. Senators such as John Warner and Charles Schumer aren't our generals, they're the janitors of our system of government. Elected officials are the housecleaners, scullery maids, cooks, dishwashers, gardeners and toilet scrubbers of our society, not the bosses or supervisors they pretend to be.

We are indeed to pray for our leaders, but let's first identify who they are. One good rule of thumb is that if they draw their pay from the public treasury, then they aren't leaders, but employees. Let's look about us at our neighbors and at the people among us who are speaking out, as you are doing. I consider you more a leader of Americans than president Bush can ever be.

I believe that our Creator has given us the form of government developed by the framers of the Articles of Confederation, the U.S. Constitution and the Confederate Constitution. If we are so ungrateful as to allow today's "public servants" to assault and rob us at will, we are insulting the great gift given to us.

To me, the gift of the American experiment in government is high on the list of gifts to humankind from our Creator. The supreme gift is, of course, salvation through our savior Jesus Christ. Our rights are a gift as well, but safeguarding those rights is a duty. We have a duty to defend the form of government designed to protect our rights. That is the duty to which General Jackson was referring.

In other words, we don't need to reinvent government in America. We need to coax it, like a reluctant stallion, back into its constitutional corral.

Our Secret Constitution

The answer, then, to our constitutional crisis lies with beliefs at the very core of our national identity. But that core requires radical surgery before it can become healthy enough to deal effectively with the country's ills. In his tour de force entitled *Our Secret Constitution*,[4] Columbia law professor George Fletcher shows how the Civil War replaced the original charter with a second American Constitution, which he calls our "secret Constitution." The Constitution of 1787 stood for a maximum freedom of expression of individual liberty, at least with regard to the federal government. The second Constitution is dedicated to organic nationhood and popular democracy, emphasizing not freedom from government but equality under the law. The state would now have to do more than leave us alone. It would have to ensure equal protection—and do it through coercion if necessary.

Professor Fletcher notes that although the original charter of 1787 officially remains in place, it has been so radically transformed by our secret Constitution that for all intents and purposes the old charter is a dead letter. Because of Lincoln's war, the Tenth Amendment was effectively abolished, the conquered states were made into puppet governments set up by the Republican Party, and Lincoln succeeded in consolidating governmental power in Washington by military dictatorship.

This means that Americans today face a choice as to whether to defend the old Constitution or to follow the new, secret charter—that is, whether to defend the concept of a limited republic with maximum freedom for the people, or to acquiesce to the new consolidated concept of power that is prone to dictatorial and imperialistic expressions. It's probably true to say that most Americans are firmly in the pro-big government camp. This includes the vast majority of Republican "conservatives." They don't mind sacrificing most of their earnings to unelected, unaccountable bureaucrats and unresponsive elected officials, nor do they mind relying on Washington for a host of taxpayer-funded benefits. And they are agreeable to the notion that personal responsibility and independence should be sacrificed for the "security" offered by politicians.

At the other end of the spectrum are people who believe in the old Constitution *verbatim* and who hold personal liberty and responsibility so dear that they dare to expect others to hold similar views. They abhor all but the most limited and narrowly defined forms of taxation because they believe their money belongs to them and that the federal government only needs enough funding to perform its few, narrowly defined constitutional duties (that is, as defined by the "old" Constitution). They want leaders who can read the plain language of the Constitution and who understand that the words "Congress shall make no law" mean Congress shall make no law.

This small but vocal group of Americans is calling for the restoration of a republic founded on the ideals of the old Constitution. They believe that the Founding Fathers designed our system of government in the form of a constitutionally limited republic with minimum government control or interference into our personal lives and business affairs. They further believe that government at all levels—federal, state, and local—was originally intended to be controlled by the people and that the Constitution explicitly restricts the power of the federal government. They are anti-interventionists and despise jingoism and imperialism, especially in the form of state-sponsored nation building.

Paleoconservatives are not isolationists. The word isolationist is a pejorative term that is used to describe anyone who does not favor using America's power and blood for their particular cause. Paleocons believe that the United States of America is the greatest nation on earth, that it should trade with all nations, and that Americans should have diplomatic contact and cultural exchange with all nations. They just don't believe in fighting foreign countries' wars or paying foreign countries' bills. That is not isolationism; that is patriotism, unalloyed by blind nationalism.

So the choice is clear. Either the old Constitution or the new, "secret" one. Either a republic or an empire. To acquiesce or not to acquiesce.

As Hamlet would say, that is the question.

— Chapter 3 —

When the Horse Dies, Dismount: The Demise of Conservatism in the Republican Party

In an essay entitled "Thank You, Tony Blair,"[5] syndicated columnist Cal Thomas defended the Bush-Blair policy on Iraq with these words:

> Saddam must be found and tried for crimes against humanity. Iraq must be rebuilt into a thriving democracy. To settle for less will invite more terrorism and more states seeking weapons to massively destroy, or at least blackmail, the United States and Britain.
>
> Blair's conclusion [during his July 17, 2003 address to Congress] sounded like an old-fashioned Fourth of July peroration: "Tell the world why you're proud of America. Tell them when 'The Star Spangled Banner' starts, Americans get to their feet. Tell them why Americans, one and all, stand upright and respectful. Not because some state official told them to, but

because whatever race, color, class or creed they are, being American means being free. That's why they're proud."

"Free" did he say? Who's kidding whom?

Today's Americans are bound by the shackles of government interference as never before, and our taskmasters are not just Democrats but Republicans. Socialism and her handmaidens, imperialism and secularism, are being promoted by the Republican Party just as much as they were ever flaunted by the Democrats. Gone forever are the days of the clear-eyed, free-market conservatism of Ronald Reagan, who actually sought to limit government, to lower taxes, to promote biblical values, and to create a climate of self-reliance and self-restraint.

Today the differences between America's two major parties are purely cosmetic. As the 2000 Constitution Party presidential candidate Howard Phillips[6] put it, the choice voters face is between two evils, adding that the Republican Party "is the greater of the two evils, because it flies a false flag." Phillips is right.

How can Americans reconcile the difference between candidate Bush who claimed to espouse traditional American values and President Bush who gave adoption rights to homosexual couples in D.C. and who appointed numerous open homosexuals to high office within his administration? What should Americans think of a president who campaigned on a promise to avoid nation building and then launched invasions of Afghanistan and Iraq? And what happened to candidate Bush's promises to practice a "humble" foreign policy? They are now scattered about like the debris of a messy divorce while the U.S. brazenly flexes its military muscle throughout the world ("Bring 'em on!").

And now the nation is learning something else about Bush that proves something is seriously amiss. It isn't just his philosophy of government but a much deeper issue his supporters have been trying to evade for years: the question of character. There is a dangerous "reality gap" between what Bush actually thinks and what he palms off on the nation. Even after the fourth or fifth attempt to pass the buck, the administration still clings to its innocence about the president's 2003 Mis-State-Ment-of-the-Union speech about Iraq's alleged nuclear capability. Little wonder the Democrats are saying that Bush has done more for the fortunes of their party than anyone could ever have dreamed possible.

At the root of Bush's troubles is not his arrogant management style or his shifty-eyed mannerisms—which are worrisome enough—but the fact that he utterly fails to represent the outlook of traditional American conservatism. Bush has touched the hot button of every ilk of conservative, from free market purists, to social issue conservatives, to right-to-lifers, to anti-tax crusaders. The Bush administration confirms everything people like Lewis Goldberg and Chuck Baldwin have been saying for years, namely that the pro-family and pro-freedom movement's fixation on the White House was a mistake. To think that simply electing George W. Bush to the White House would somehow solve our country's problems was the height of folly.

The lesson should be obvious. If conservatives want to control *their* homes, *their* children's education, and *their* most cherished freedoms, they must throw out once and for all the myth of Republican conservatism and demand leaders who will be true to their oath to protect and defend the Constitution. This is one of the reasons we are beginning to hear new voices from Middle America telling us that there is right and wrong, that there is hope to restore the Constitution, and that the values this nation was founded upon are still worth fighting for. Their message to the American people is plain: The tide is turning. However dark the days may seem, voices of hope and renewal are rising even now. All across this great land of ours the chimes of freedom are ringing louder and clearer.

How Bush Survives

Meanwhile an important question remains: How much longer are Christians going to give President Bush a pass for his unconstitutional actions? How *does* he survive? In my opinion, Bush gets away with his usurpations largely because the evangelical public views him as a sincere and earnest Christian. Christianity has come to be identified with the state in such a way that would have shocked the earliest Christians. How did this fundamental transition take place?

The sharp distinction between the pre- and post-Constantinian church may help us to answer this question. Tertullian (150-220), an early Christian apologist, argued that if law was not based on justice it was tyranny. He affirmed a strong notion of conscientious commitment to the "good," even if that meant disobeying a law. As he wrote in his *Apology*, "If I have found what your law prohibits to be good...has it not lost its power to debar me from it?" He furthermore insisted that a law is not only to be justly administered, it must be seen to be just by those who were expected to obey it: "...it is not enough that a law is just, nor that a judge should be convinced of its justice; those from whom obedience is expected should have that conviction too."

Unlike President Bush and the current neocon establishment in Washington, Tertullian affirmed a sharp distinction between the divine and human spheres. "As the divine and human are ever opposed to each other, when we are condemned by you [the state], we are acquitted by the Highest." Ultimately, it was this kind of radical obedience to God that formed the basis of Tertullian's response to the state. It led to the sort of uncompromising resistance and a measure of indifference to the complexities of civil rule that today characterize Roy Moore's stance in the Alabama Ten Commandments case.

The contrast between Tertullian's *Apology* and Eusebius's (260-337) panegyric written to celebrate the thirtieth anniversary of

Constantine's reign on July 25, 335 is remarkable. Constantine had become the supreme ruler in the West, having seen (according to tradition) the sign of the cross in the sky with the words *In hoc signo vinces*, "in this sign you will conquer." Largely as the result of a series of bloody and treacherous deeds, he had become the sole ruler of the empire and had made Christianity its official religion. It was at this point that a fundamental shift in the church's perception of the state took place and a new attitude toward political power was assumed by Christians.

Although Eusebius never acknowledged the emperor as divine, he regarded him as more than a mere mortal. In his "Oration in Praise of the Emperor Constantine Pronounced on the Thirtieth Anniversary of His Reign," he came to view the emperor as the favored one whom God "receives," "a transcript of divine sovereignty," "an imitation of God himself," a representative of the divine Logos who "reigns from ages which had no beginning." He was a "friend of God" and "an interpreter of the Word of God," one who frames "his earthly government according to the pattern of that divine original, feeling strength in its conformity to the Monarchy of God."

Thus with the rise of Constantine a decisively new phase of church-state relationships had been reached. The political implications of the early church's radical monotheism were cast aside, the monarchy was sacralized, and the church elevated civil authority to a status not hitherto known within Christianity. Note carefully that this was *not* the result of official persecution by the state. On the contrary, it was the church's *willing* theological legitimation of Constantine that sealed its political captivity.

This close relationship between church and state may well be the ultimate reason why so many evangelical Christians excuse the unconstitutional federalization of our country, a process that has only increased in celerity since the Bush administration came to power. But the ideological foundation was laid in the fourth century. Since that time the concept of political rule—and blind obeisance by the public—would enjoy a theological legitimation against which opponents of a particular civil authority could only prevail in the most extenuating circumstances.

Tertullian of Carthage was not primarily interested in political renewal at all. He simply wanted a government that would leave the church to affirm its obedience to God without unnecessary interference from the state. It was this *theological* commitment that led to *political* confrontation between the church and the Roman state. The highest loyalty that Tertullian believed he could bring to the state was to convince it that its authority was under God and that it therefore was accountable to Him. As Alistair Kee has noted, "Constantine achieved by kindness what his predecessors had not been able to achieve by force. Without a threat or a blow, and all unsuspecting, the Christians were led into captivity and their religion transformed into a new imperial cult."

Schwarzenegger: Bad Actor, Worse Governor

The strange case of Arnold Schwarzenegger, California's latest governor, is a good example of Republican conservatism sacrificed on the altar of expediency. I used to think that the best joke about Arnold Schwarzenegger was David Letterman's late-night quip. He said the number one Arnold Schwarzenegger campaign promise was to "Speak directly to voters in clear, honest, broken English." I've changed my mind, however, since reading the flurry of support for Schwarzenegger coming from conservative Republicans, many of whom are evangelical Christians.

That evangelicals could even discuss whether or not to support Schwarzenegger shows just how willing they are to compromise their principles when it comes to political elections. This is the philosophy that says Christian values don't really matter in the political system. "Sure, Schwarzenegger is not as conservative as we'd like, but he's a Republican—and that's gotta be better than having a Democrat as governor!" Indeed, Schwarzenegger won the California recall election due largely to Republican voters who placed pragmatism over principle.

Prior to the election, I posted a letter to Californians on my website. (Having lived in Southern California for 27 years, I felt I had the right to speak out.) My message to evangelical voters in California was this. If you want to choose as your next governor a pro-abortion, pro-homosexual, and anti-Second Amendment candidate, go right ahead. If you want to vote for a man who in a 1977 interview admitted taking part in group sex, have at it. If you want to confuse economic success (which Schwarzenegger certainly has achieved) with knowledge of the Constitution and biblical law, you are certainly free to do so. Just forget that the man you're voting for has killed more than 300 people on screen, or that he has posed for nude photos, or that he supports gun control, or that he once compared weight-lifting with sex, or that he would allow women to continue killing their babies. After all, a *Republican* governor is needed in California! On the other hand, if you want a candidate who will restore morality, ethics, and common sense to public service, you'll have to look elsewhere. If you seek a politician who will return our Constitution to its proper place in our republic, you'll have to look elsewhere. If you believe in an individual's constitutional right to keep and bear arms, you'll have to look elsewhere. If you believe that a doctor, when treating a pregnant woman, has *two* patients—the mother and the unborn baby—you'll have to look elsewhere. And in this case, "looking elsewhere" may mean not voting at all if that means compromising your Christian values.

Rev. Louis P. Sheldon, chairman of the Traditional Values Coalition, stated that Arnold Schwarzenegger would create a "moral vacuum" in Sacramento if he became California's governor.[7] "As Governor, Mr. Schwarzenegger would be a darker villain than any he has faced in his movies. And when it comes to the moral issues that Californians really care about—he gives us inaction not action." In other words, bad actor, worse governor. Why evangelicals should still need proof that the Republican Party has sold its soul for election-day pottage is beyond me. But if you're one who still holds to the lesser-of-two-evils philosophy, take a good hard look at the California recall election—and the support the Terminator received from "conservative" Christians.

The Reinvention of Elizabeth Dole

The election of Elizabeth Dole to the U.S. Senate should be just as disturbing to true conservatives as the results of the California recall election. In the 2002 elections most of my conservative friends got what they wanted—a Republican victory in the North Carolina senatorial race. They were sure that Liddy Dole would stand up for their conservative values. After all, she's a Republican, isn't she?

Those who rushed to join the Liddy bandwagon might want to pause. "We are skeptical, very skeptical, that Dole will carry out the mantle of Jesse Helms," said Lori Waters,[8] executive director of the Eagle Forum, a group headed by conservative columnist Phyllis Schlafly. "She's had a history of making some not so conservative statements. Having Jesse Helms as a standard is very hard to live up to. We're not optimistic that she would be able to meet that standard." So while my friends are celebrating Dole's victory, there are a few things they may want to consider—or forget.

•   Forget that her 1999 presidential campaign was a joke and that *National Review* magazine urged her to run as a Democrat in a story titled "Gore-Dole 2000—A Place for Mrs. D." And while you're at it, forget that she was in and out of the presidential campaign in about 90 days, before she was forced to give detailed position statements, even though her history suggests that she has either refused to take a stand or has acquiesced to liberal policies in organizations she has led during her nearly forty years in public life. After all, she's a Republican.

- Forget the radical policies and theology espoused by her former congregation, the Foundry Church, which was also attended by the Clintons.

- Forget that for nearly four years the Doles listened to anti-free enterprise, pro-abortion, and pro-gay agenda sermons, apparently without feeling uncomfortable. Forget that they left the church only when media exposure forced them to do so. After all, she's a Republican.

- Forget that as Transportation Secretary under Ronald Reagan she supported maintaining the intrusive 55 miles per hour federal law even though research showed that her efforts to delay the overturn of the 55 mph rule cost thousands of highway fatalities.

- Forget that she promoted the Equal Rights Amendment, contrary to the Reagan administration's agenda.

- Forget that as Labor Secretary under Bush she went on an anti-business crusade, vastly enlarging the power of OSHA to harass businesses.

- Forget that she supported "glass ceiling" laws that are used to harass and litigate against the private sector for not having the "proper" ratio of women in certain positions.

- Forget that she supported the Job Training Partnership Act (JTPA), one of the biggest wastes of taxpayers' dollars ever.

- Forget that she empowered labor unions by refusing to notify workers about their right to refuse payment of dues used for political purposes, allowing organized labor to continue collecting millions of dollars from unsuspecting workers.

- Forget that she initiated the SCANS Commission that created the Goals 2000/School-to-Work movement, a movement that has severely dumbed down our public schools and has undermined the teaching of basic academic skills.

- Forget that her mismanagement as president of the American Red Cross resulted in thousands of health and safety code violations, causing the Food and Drug Administration to essentially take control of the agency via consent decree.

- Forget that she used the ARC to promote the homosexual agenda by sending Red Cross lobbyists and lawyers around the country to oppose common sense AIDS bills that attempted to curtail the spread of that disease.

- Forget that she has declared herself "pro-life" but has consistently refused to go into greater detail on such questions as when life begins and on the role of government funding of groups (such as the ARC) that promote "safe sex" education programs.

- Forget that while running for president in 1999 she called for a ban on a large class of semi-automatic rifles, restrictions on ammunition, and mandatory trigger locks—all of which would have severely restricted ordinary citizens from being able to defend themselves.

- Forget that before running for office she hadn't lived in North Carolina in 40 years except for periodical visits to her mother, whose Salisbury residence Dole now claims as her own.

Here's my point. In the end it really doesn't matter in the least that the Republicans won control of the Senate. Government will continue to get bigger, more intrusive, and less efficient. And since a Republican Congress will expand government at just about the same speed as a Democratic Congress, a vote for a Republican candidate won't change a thing.

It's mind-boggling how many conservatives defend Republican politicians regardless of their actions. They've fallen for the lie that Democrats are worse than Republicans. In truth, it was more dangerous for conservatives to vote for Elizabeth Dole than for her Democrat rival, Erskine Bowles. Dole will not only get away with promoting new federal programs, she will also have free rein to expand existing Democrat programs with virtually no opposition whatsoever from conservatives.

In 1995, Republicans promised that the National Endowment of the Arts would be abolished. Conservatives cheered. But when the Republicans couldn't conjure up enough votes to put their plan into action, they hastily retreated. William Bennett of Empower America asked, "If the Republican Party will retreat on this issue, where will they stand firm?" In response, Steve Dasbach of the Libertarian Party said: "The Republican Party won't stand firm anywhere. When it comes to consistency, the GOP is the political equivalent of Jell-O."

In the end, I'm not surprised that my conservative friends voted for Elizabeth Dole. Like her husband Bob, Mrs. Dole has become a master pitchman. Bob has successfully made a post-political career hawking Viagra and becoming weepy over veterans' causes. And I bet you a Texas peso that Liddy will be as successful in her new role as the conservatives' Joan of Arc.

After all, she's a Republican.

The Greater of Two Evils

Both Schwarzenegger and Dole illustrate the fact that our federal Constitution is a dead letter to most politicians. Our two-party system only encourages this negligence. George Wallace once said there wasn't a "dime's worth of difference" between the two major parties. More recently, Pat Buchanan called them the "two wings of the same bird of prey."

In truth, both liberals and neoconservatives are cut from the same cloth. Both ask, "Who's going to control Big Brother?" instead of asking (as they should), "How can we get rid of Big Brother?" The only real difference between liberals and conservatives is that they devise different plans on what to do with the power of the federal government. That's why Republicans have failed to prevent the growth of the federal budget in recent years, for they aren't even faintly interested in controlling the expansion of government. Neither liberal nor conservative politicians are willing to get to the heart of the problem—the question of the legitimate use of government power. As George Washington warned, "Government is not reason, it is not eloquence—it is force. Like fire it is a dangerous servant and a fearful master; never for a moment should it be left to irresponsible action." Yet our politicians produce their plans and programs without ever being challenged on the immoral and unethical means they use.

The story is told of a skyscraper that had just been built when a crack was discovered on the 72nd story. The owners brought in the original engineers, who took the elevator to the third sub-basement where they found the problem. Friends, our problems in America are much deeper than we think. In the name of "ethics" we have unethically disregarded the proper separation of church and state by transferring to the state the obligations that God has laid upon His church. Meanwhile, we seem content to debate the cracks on the 72nd story and ignore the real problem in the third sub-basement.

As I have frequently argued, the problem of the size of government is not really a political problem at all, but a spiritual, moral, and ethical one. I believe it's time to stop discussing the pros and cons of government programs and to come to terms with the fact that *the power of the federal government is out of control.* This doesn't make me any less compassionate than my Republican friends. Christians have a moral and Scriptural obligation to help the needy. But if history has taught us anything, it is that the solution to the problem of human need is not the intervention and compulsive agency of the state to improve the outward economic circumstances of the poor. There is nothing "compassionate" about robbing hard-working people of their incomes to help others. To advocate such an approach is to deny the clear teaching of God's Word because it abandons the gracious character of Christian charity.

It's easy to forget the foundational concept upon which our society was built, namely that government officials are under an obligation to be guided by the principles of divine law. And it was the distinct purpose of the federal Constitution to limit, not the power of the people, but the power of government. The Founders argued that unless the federal government was bound by the chains of the Constitution, it would inevitably develop into a monstrous Leviathan through uncontrolled growth. Tragically, that is exactly what has happened in our nation.

When the state oversteps its authority, there are two things we can do. The first is to swallow our pride and acknowledge that as a society we have unwisely permitted our elected officials to base their policies on humanly devised guidelines instead of on biblical ones. The second is to call for a return to the law of God as the supreme and sole standard for determining the legitimate function of government. This means (among other things) that Christian politicians, many of whom are political conservatives and evangelicals, must acknowledge that they have promoted ethically commendable goals by unethical means in calling upon the state to exercise its power of compulsion where there is no biblical warrant for it. The Founders of our great nation understood that the best government is always the least government. It is even better when it is accountable to "We the People." As Circuit Justice William Paterson wrote in 1795:

> What is a Constitution? It is the form of government, delineated by the mighty hand of the people, in which certain first principles of fundamental laws are established. The Constitution is certain and fixed; it contains the permanent will of the people, and is the supreme law of the land; it is paramount to the

power of the Legislature, and can be revoked or altered only by the authority that made it. The life-giving principle and the death-doing stroke must proceed from the same hand. What are Legislatures? Creatures of the Constitution; they owe their existence to the Constitution: they derive their powers from the Constitution: It is their commission; and, therefore, all their acts must be conformable to it, or else they will be void. The Constitution is the work or will of the People themselves, in their original, sovereign, and unlimited capacity. Law is the work or will of the Legislature in their derivative and subordinate capacity. The one is the work of the Creator, and the other of the Creature. The Constitution fixes limits to the exercise of legislative authority, and prescribes the orbit within which it must move. In short, gentlemen, the Constitution is the sun of the political system, around which all Legislative, Executive and Judicial bodies must revolve.

The next election will be all about restoring that accountability to the Constitution. However, unless voters get serious about constitutional government, Democrats and Republicans will go on their merry way sharing power, and our society will continue to go on its accustomed path—"slouching toward Gomorrah," as Robert Bork once put it. Voters will continue to be content to choose whichever party they consider to be the "lesser of two evils." Never mind that neither party is committed to paying anything other than lip service to recovering our biblical and constitutional bearings! Although the Second Amendment clearly states that the right of the people to bear arms "shall not be infringed," our good politicians will continue to find ways to dance around the word "not." They will continue to disregard the first guarantee of the Declaration of Independence—the right to life—meaning that the unborn child has a fundamental individual right that cannot be infringed. They will continue to seek to placate the homosexual lobby in order to expand their political base. They will continue to make decisions on assisted suicide that have broad, Roe v. Wade-like implications even while supporting activist judges who usurp the power of the people with decisions that stem more from political correctness than constitutional authority. In short, they will continue to put pragmatism over principle as they unleash torrents of political correctness, radical feminism, anti-intellectualism, and affirmative action on society.

The next time you vote, ask yourself the question: What's the difference in God's eyes between "evil" and "completely evil"? The only difference between the GOP and Democrats is the degree of evil they support. Do you really believe that God would have you vote for a party that knowingly consents to the continuation of 1.5 million abortions per year and that will appoint judges to decree that Roe v. Wade is legitimate? Am I the only one who thinks there's an alternative to the brutal dehumanizing calculations of the socialism that pervades our land or to the materialistic worship of the state that big government brings us?

Thomas Paine once said, "Moderation in temper is a virtue, but moderation in principle is always a vice." I urge Americans to set a higher standard than they've ever set before. If we continue in our pragmatism, we will get what we deserve—men-pleasers instead of God-fearers. Let's elect people who are humble enough to submit to the supreme law of the land, the U.S. Constitution. If we don't, the current batch of spoiled intellectuals and starry-eyed executives will continue to wreak havoc upon the land of the free with their radical egalitarian ideas and ethic of unlimited personal hedonism.

If you had asked me in 2000 whether I thought voting for a third party candidate could make a significant impact on the political scene, I would have said no. As Lew Rockwell observes,[9] "The spectacle of elections grows more absurd every year. We are asked to cast ballots for people we do not know because they make promises they are under no obligation to keep. What's even worse, the voting gesture is pointless on the margin. The chances that any one vote (meaning your vote) will actually have an impact are so infinitesimally small as to be meaningless."

Nevertheless, I haven't given up on the viability of third party candidacies. My sense is that millions of Americans deeply believe it is time to forge a new coalition. Voters are fed up with the two main parties. They are also much more independent-minded about the quality of life they want for themselves and their families. The time is ripe for real change. Jesse Ventura proved it when he upset two highly financed political machines in Minnesota. Whatever the reasons—fallout from years of abusing the Constitution, the hubris of our politicians, or the general unease brought on by America's foreign policy—voters are suddenly open to new voices, new ideas, new leadership. And remember, only about one third of all eligible voters bothered to vote in the last presidential election. All this leaves a huge number of people looking for a reason to vote.

Our Next President?

Clearly the time has come for a new kind of leader in America. What would our next president be like if Americans did an about-face and returned to constitutional principles?

• He would be a man of devotion to good government, which by definition is limited constitutional government, and to the freedoms of individuals as guaranteed by the Bill of Rights and secured to them by the Ninth and Tenth Amendments.

• He would be a man who unquestioningly supports the Constitution—a document that William Gladstone once described as the most wonderful work ever struck off at a given time by the brain and purpose of man—which protects all American citizens from tyranny on the one hand and anarchy on the other.

- He would be a man who recognizes that a government that is not a government of laws is a despotism; that occupants of public offices love power and are prone to abuse it; and that the Founders desired above all else to secure to the people in a written Constitution every right that they had wrested from autocratic rulers while they were struggling for the right of self-rule and freedom.

- He would be a man who recognizes that rights come from God Himself and are therefore unalienable, i.e., they cannot be taken away; that the possession of these rights is absolutely necessary for a free society; and that violation of these rights by government is nothing less than tyranny.

- He would be a man who understands that the supreme duty of government as envisioned by our Foundersis to defend the Constitution and to oppose all enactments that violate the supreme law of the land; that it is therefore improper to approve funds for any federal agency, program, or activity that is not specifically authorized by the Constitution; and that it is time to reduce the size of the federal government by abolishing or returning to the states all departments, agencies, or programs lacking constitutionally granted authority.

- He would be a man who understands that it is not the proper role of government to take money from one wage earner and transfer that wealth to another.

- He would be a man who understands that all teaching is related to basic assumptions about God and man; that education cannot be separated from religious faith; that God's law assigns the authority and responsibility of educating children to their parents; and that education should therefore be free from all federal government subsidies, including vouchers, tax incentives, and loans.

- He would be a man who understands that the right to keep and bear arms is inherent in the right of self-defense conferred on the individual and the community by God to safeguard life, liberty, and property; that this right is guaranteed by the Second Amendment to the Constitution; and that it may not properly be infringed upon or denied.

- He would be a man who recognizes that the Constitution speaks with finality, and that the oath of Supreme Court Justices to support it is worse than mockery if they do not discharge their duties agreeably to the Constitution.

- He would be a man who recognizes that the most serious threat to good government and freedom in America is not posed by evil-minded men and women but by legislative and judicial activists who are bent on remaking America in the image of their own New World thinking.

- He would be a man who rejects the devastating school of economics that promises abundance for all by robbing selected Peters to pay collective Paul, a man who teaches that earth yields nothing to man except the products of his own labor and that free men cannot be induced to provide goods or services of value unless they are allowed to retain a fair share of the fruits of their labor for themselves, their families, and the causes they hold dear.

- He would be man who believes that participation in the United Nations is fundamentally incompatible with American sovereignty and the Constitution.

- He would be a man who will refuse to surrender our precious independence through trade agreements and organizations like the WTO and NAFTA.

- He would be a man who believes in a strong national defense and who would never sacrifice freedom or violate the Constitution for so-called "security."

- He would be a man who recognizes that only Congress has the constitutional authority to declare war.

- He would be a man whose predominant characteristics are his personal integrity and humility.

Two centuries ago George Washington was the inevitable and unchallenged choice for president of the newly founded republic. He did not seek the office and was reluctant to accept it. He was uncertain of his ability to discharge the duties that would devolve upon him and was more than ready to retire to his beloved Mount Vernon after the exertions of the Revolutionary War. But the unanimous call of his countrymen was hardly less than a command to a man of his character and love of country.

Whether a new George Washington awaits us beyond the stormy horizon I do not know. Only time will tell if America will decide to return to her biblical and constitutional roots. But it is my fervent hope and prayer that she does.

— Chapter 4 —

Confederate Flags, American History, and Yankee Myths: How Lincoln's War Changed America Forever

When state officials in Missouri took down Confederate flags at two historic sites after congressman Richard Gephardt said they shouldn't be flown anywhere in America, Steven Greenhut wrote in LewRockwell.com:[10] "Why aren't more people outraged when Democratic congressman and Presidential candidate Dick Gephardt, D-Missouri, said 'the Confederate flag no longer has a place flying anytime, anywhere in our great nation'? What right does he have to tell South Carolina what flag to hoist on the statehouse grounds, or to tell me what to fly in my own yard? If Americans had any courage, rebel flags would pop up everywhere just to spite him."

Well, I did Mr. Greenhut one better. I sent Dick Gephardt a flag—a large Third National Flag of the Confederacy. I also sent him a letter containing the following sentiments.[11]

Mr. Gephardt, I proudly fly the flag you disdain, and I do it for one reason: to protest the federal bureaucracy you represent. It symbolizes the fact that the United States of America was formed as just that—a union of sovereign states into what is known as a federal government. The concept behind our government was simple. Our "Creator" gave each of us "unalienable rights," out of which we in turn gave limited rights to our respective state governments. Then the states gave in turn a portion of their rights to a central government that could perform certain wide-ranging tasks such as national defense and the conduct of foreign relations. The framers of our Constitution were careful to make it clear that the powers not granted to the federal government were reserved to the states and ultimately to "We the People."

Mr. Gephardt, people ask us here in the South, "What do you want?" I say it's really not so wild a dream. All we want is the restoration of a constitutional republic that the Founding Fathers established in this country. They didn't have in mind some gigantic federal bureaucracy with all this power and control regulating our lives and our businesses. They had in mind a federal government that would abide by the Tenth Amendment. It was small, it had limited powers, it took care of national events, and it defended our borders. They maintained the army and issued national currency. And all the rest of the rights and responsibilities, they said, belonged to the states, respectively, and the people.

As Robert E. Lee put it, "All that the South has ever desired was that the Union as established by our forefathers should be preserved, and that the government as originally organized should be administered in purity and truth."

> Above all, we reject the notion of "salvation by society": the belief that society…will lead individuals to spiritual perfection, and this through the ministrations of more and bigger government.
>
> The media have already shown where they will put their support—not behind the people but behind big government. But common sense is on the march.
>
> Please do not return the flag if you don't want it. I already have plenty. I can't imagine you throwing it in the trash, either. Perhaps you can just give it to Senator Lieberman—oops, he hates the flag too!

As you can see, I can get a bit cantankerous when it comes to Yankee snobbery. I've taken more than a little heat for having published columns suggesting—goodness, has it come to this?—that the South is not the evil, wicked, vile place the PC crowd says it is. In case any of you pro-Lincoln types might be reading this book, let me be as candid as possible. As a former resident of Hawaii and California who has lived in the South for a number of years, I have very little tolerance for Northern sanctimony or, for that matter, "Southerners" who trip over themselves trying to grovel at the feet of the Cultural Marxists. Despite what the PC hatemongers say, displaying a Confederate flag doesn't indicate a lack of allegiance to the United States. I am an American and proud of it. And in my opinion, anybody who hates tyranny should love that flag, too. Seeing the Stars and Bars waving reminds me of how fortunate I am to be an adopted son of the South, whose heroes include such godly Christians as Jefferson Davis, "Stonewall" Jackson, Robert Dabney, Basil Manly, John Broadus, and—last but certainly not least—Robert E. Lee.

Did you know that it's only been in the last 15 years or so that the Confederate flag has acquired a racist reputation? That is, only since this PC nonsense began sweeping the country. You know something else? By using the same stupid argument the PC crowd uses to claim that the Confederate flag is racist you can make the same claim about the Stars and Stripes. Slavery was an institution in this country for at least 200 years before the Confederacy was founded and for 100 years under the American flag. It was the American flag that hung from the masts of the New England slave ships that brought the Africans to America by the thousands. American flags and Christian crosses outnumber Confederate flags 100 to 1 in photos of KKK rallies. So if you want to be offended by a flag, be offended by the American flag.

The sad truth is that detractors of the Confederate flag have little or no concept of American history. The Yankee myth of a righteous North and an evil South is just that—a myth. Steven Yates[12] summarizes it well:

> It is always useful to remember that one of the chief aims of tolerance totalitarianism is to rewrite history, to force this entire country—and this means every institution in it—to embrace a politically correct, cultural Marxist paradigm of history and culture. In this version of history and culture, central to U.S. history has been the struggle of the victims (blacks, women, etc.) against their oppressors (white men). In this simplistic model, slavery was the only cause of the War Between the States. Never mind those pesky details about tariffs or centralization. One of the ways totalitarians gain and maintain power is to control the information that reaches people—be it through education or the media or, when those fail, threats, intimidation, or the banishing of a Maurice Bessinger from the "polite society" of the tolerant. This must include what symbols are allowed public display. Those who associate the Confederate flag with something called states rights—and associate that not with race but with limitations on a powerful, central

government—have long been thorns in the side of those who want to build up that kind of government.

A book everyone needs to read is *When in the Course of Human Events: Arguing the Case for Southern Secession*.[13] It shows how the Civil War destroyed America as the Founders intended it to be—a decentralized federal system—and opened the floodgates for the vast centralized empire we have today. The author, Charles Adams, shows that in order to legitimate this revolutionary change, Americans had to be taught a plethora of lies, among them that secession was unconstitutional, that the South seceded to protect slavery, and that the North invaded the South to emancipate slaves. Nothing could be further from the truth. Adams shows how the war was fought over control of territory, resources, and revenue.

I invite my pro-Yankee friends to read Adams' book. You'll realize just how much you've got to learn about Lincoln's war—as I did. *Then* come and talk to me. Meanwhile, throwing a racism charge or something similar against a person who makes a politically unpopular but principled stand for liberty and the Constitution may be the way things are done here in America, but it doesn't make it right.

Was Secession Treason?

America was founded on a revolution against England, yet many Americans now believe the myth that secession was treasonable. The Declaration of Independence was, in fact, a declaration of secession. Its final paragraph declares inarguably the ultimate sovereignty of each state:

> [T]hat these united colonies are, and of right ought to be free and independent states; that they are absolved of all allegiance to the British Crown, and that all political connection between them and the State of Great Britain, is and ought to be totally dissolved; and that as free and independent states, they have full power to levy war, conclude peace, contract alliances, establish commerce, and to do all other acts and things which independent states may of right do.

Following the Declaration of Independence, each colony established by law the legitimacy of its own sovereignty as a state. Each one drew up, voted upon, and then ratified its own state constitution, which declared and defined its sovereignty as a state. Realizing that they could not survive upon the world stage as thirteen individual sovereign nations, the states then joined together formally into a confederation of states, but only for the purposes of negotiating treaties, waging war, and regulating foreign commerce.

For those specific purposes the thirteen states adopted the Articles of Confederation in 1781, thus creating the United States of America. The Articles of Confederation spelled out clearly where the real power lay. Article II said, "Each state retains its sovereignty, freedom, and independence, and every power, jurisdiction, and right, which is not by this confederation expressly delegated to the United States, in Congress assembled." The Article also prohibited the secession of any member state ("the union shall be perpetual," Article XIII) unless all of the states agreed to dissolve the Articles.

Six years later, the Constitutional Convention was convened in Philadelphia, supposedly to overhaul the Articles. However, the delegates in Philadelphia decided to scrap the Articles and to propose to the states a different charter—the United States Constitution. Its purpose was to retain the sovereignty of the states but to delegate to the United States government a few more powers than the Articles had granted it. One major difference between the two charters was that the Constitution made no mention of "perpetual union," and it did not contain any prohibition against the secession of states from the union. The point was raised in the convention: Should there be a "perpetual union" clause in the Constitution? The delegates voted it down, and the states were left free to secede under the Constitution, which remains the U.S. government charter today.

After the election of Thomas Jefferson, the Federalist Party in New England was so upset that for more than ten years they plotted to secede. The party actually held a secession convention in Hartford, Connecticut, in 1814. Although they ultimately decided not to leave the Union, nobody really questioned the fundamental right of secession. In fact, the leader of the whole movement, Massachusetts Senator Timothy Pickering, said that secession was *the* principle of the American Revolution. Even John Quincy Adams, who was a staunch unionist, said in an 1839 speech about secession that in "dissolving that which can no longer bind, we would have to leave the separated parts to be reunited by the law of political gravitation to the center." Likewise, Alexander Hamilton stated, "to coerce the states is one of the maddest projects that was ever devised." These men, and many others, understood that there was a right of secession, and that the federal government would have no right to force any state to remain in the Union.

Some people see the Confederates as traitors to their nation because many Confederate leaders swore to protect and defend the Constitution of the United States when joining the United States Army. However, at that time people were citizens of individual states that were members of the United States, so that when a state seceded, the citizens of that state were no longer affiliated with the national government. Remember, the Constitution did not create an all-powerful national democracy, but rather a confederation of sovereign states. The existence of the Electoral College, the Bill of Rights, and the United States Senate clearly shows this; and although it is frequently ignored, the Tenth Amendment specifically states that the rights not given to the federal government are the rights of the states and of the people. But if states do not have the right to secede, they have no rights at all. Lincoln's war destroyed the government of our Founding Fathers by the "might makes right" method, a method the Republicans used to quash Confederates and loyal Democrats alike.

After the war, Jefferson Davis, the President of the Confederacy, was arrested and placed in prison prior to a trial. The trial was never held because the chief justice of the Supreme Court, Mr. Salmon Portland Chase, informed President Andrew Johnson that if Davis were placed on trial for treason the United States would lose the case because nothing in the Constitution forbids secession. That is why no trial of Jefferson Davis was held, despite the fact that he wanted one.

So was secession treason? The answer is clearly no.

Outrage at Point Lookout

The price paid by the Confederacy for defending its constitutional rights was enormous. An example of this is what took place at the Union POW camp at Point Lookout, Maryland, where a memorial service is held annually. The event is organized by the Point Lookout Prisoners-of-War Association. Present are reenactors, vendors, and descendants of prisoners.

Attending the 2003 service were several speakers, though these were limited to those vetted by the U.S. Department of Veterans Affairs, which insisted that the activities and messages be "viewpoint neutral." Earlier, a federal judge had rebuffed one speaker's efforts to enjoin the VA from censoring his intended remarks at the ceremony. The speaker's prospective offense? Criticizing the VA's flag policy, which allows the Confederate banner to fly there only one day a year during the annual memorial event. The speaker gave his talk anyway, sans the offensive passage.

The federal restrictions on speech during the memorial service were sorry enough, but the story of the camp itself is absolutely mind-boggling. During the two-year span of operation at Point Lookout, the camp saw approximately 52,000 Confederate POWs pass through its gates—military and civilian, men, women, even children. The youngest POW at Point Lookout was Baby Perkins, who was born there. His mother had been captured at the Battle of Spotsylvania with her artillery unit.

Prison conditions were, to put it mildly, deplorable. According to numerous eyewitness reports and other publications, the prisoners were forced to discard anything bearing the initials "U.S.," which for almost all Confederates meant more than half of their belongings. Only one blanket was permitted among sixteen or more men who were crowded into threadbare Sibley tents. Firewood and the essentials for health and comfort were scarce. Below-minimal rations caused scurvy and malnutrition. Lice, disease, and chronic diarrhea often resulted in an infectious death. According to one account, Confederate Sergeant Charles T. Loehr, captured at the battle of Five Forks, received a rude awakening his first night at the camp. He was one of forty men placed in a tent designed for sixteen. Six or seven of the forty had died by morning, including the two on either side of Loehr. Loehr wrote that his captors were "of the worst sort and very brutal; when the prisoners were driven out of their tents at night by diarrhea, the guards would make them carry them on their back; they were quick-stepped about the grounds, forced to kneel and pray for Abe Lincoln, etc."

Prisoners ate rats and raw fish. One hungry prisoner devoured a raw seagull that had been washed ashore. Soap skim and trash peelings were often consumed. Prisoners had no shoes in winter. High water often flooded the tents in the camp area. The undrained marshes bred mosquitoes. Malaria, typhoid fever, and smallpox were common. The brackish water supply was contaminated by unsanitary camp conditions. Prisoners were randomly shot during the night as they slept or if they called out from pain. Federal authorities refused to permit Marylanders to aid the inmates with the bare necessities of life, and thousands of prisoners died for lack of food, medical care, or proper sanitary conditions. Moreover, the head of the camp, Provost Marshall (Major) A.G. Brady, personally made in excess of $1,000,000 during his time as camp commander by pilfering clothing and other necessities of life.

Amazingly, the federal government lists only 3,384 names that are inscribed on the monument plaques. However, according to prisoners' diaries and other reports, over 14,000 prisoners died while incarcerated in the camp. Only one "unknown" soldier is listed on the monument, yet absent are 413 additional *confirmed* names of those who died at Point Lookout. When the prisoners' remains were moved from Tanner's Creek to the present cemetery, their skulls were put in one box, the arm bones in another, and the leg bones in a third box. The men who moved them were paid in accordance with the number of skull bones. Frequently they would gamble with the skulls, and bones were dropped and left in the road. Children walking to school would pick them up, not knowing what they were, and take them to class for show-and-tell.

In its living conditions and treatment of prisoners, Point Lookout has often been compared to Andersonville, the Confederate prison for Union troops in Georgia. Such comparisons are to be taken *cum grano salis*. The mortality rate at Point Lookout was greater than that of the Confederate prison at Andersonville. Moreover, the fatalities at Point Lookout were due to unnecessary neglect, while those at Andersonville were due to a real want in the Confederacy as a whole. The United States War Department's official statistics showed that more Southern prisoners died in Northern camps than did Northern soldiers in Southern camps. The death rate in Northern camps was approximately twelve percent, while the death rate in Southern camps was about nine percent. The people of the South were starving by the end of the war and couldn't feed their own troops, but the North had no such excuse.

Keep in mind that the Confederate government did everything possible to exchange prisoners with the North. In 1863, Union Secretary of War Stanton decided to end prisoner exchanges on the grounds that the South had more to gain than the North. Even when the South explained its increasing inability to care for the prisoners,

Stanton refused to resume the exchanges. Captain Wirz, the commandant at Andersonville, allowed a party of four prisoners to go to Washington on parole to explain the hardships at Andersonville and plead for an exchange. The men saw Stanton but were unsuccessful in convincing him to the exchange. The men returned to Andersonville and in post-war accounts condemned Stanton for his refusal to allow prisoner exchanges. In February of 1865, Wirz released 3,000 prisoners who were well enough to travel on their own to the Federal base in Jacksonville, Florida. The Union commander refused to accept them, and they were returned to Andersonville. Yet the myth of Southern brutality continues.

Lincoln's War: Just Conflict or Tyrannical Crusade?

In a *Blueprint Magazine* article entitled "How to Fight a Just War," Jean Bethke Elshtain wrote:[14] "On Sept. 11, America sustained a greater loss of human life in a single day than ever before in our history, easily topping the previous norm for one day of death, the Battle of Antietam."

Having participated in the 2002 Antietam battle reenactment in Maryland—and being "mortally wounded" in the Sunken Road—I would remind readers that the total number of dead for the September 17, 1862, clash was 3,650 soldiers, a sum larger than the 3,044 people who perished on 9/11. Antietam battle deaths included 2,100 Union and 1,550 Confederate combatants. No one knows the actual number of men who died later as a result of their wounds or the number of missing who had been killed. If you take a conservative estimate of 20 percent of the wounded dying of their wounds and 30 percent of the missing killed, the approximate number of soldiers who died as a result of this battle are 7,640—or about 4,600 more than died on September 11, 2001.

Were these deaths really necessary? Could they have been avoided? Was, in fact, the Civil War a necessary conflict in the first place? To answer these questions, it may be helpful to look at what is called just war theory. This theory is comprised of two main themes: *jus ad bellum*, or the just reasons to go to war, and *jus in bello*, or the just conduct of war. The first Christian thinker to write extensively about the subject was St. Augustine in the fifth century. These principles answer two basic questions:

(a) What are the principles for becoming engaged in a just war?

1. Just cause. The cause of initiating the war must be just. Just causes might include the vindication of justice, the protection of innocent human life, or the restoration of basic human rights.
2. Competent authority. War can be initiated justly only by those who hold the requisite authority for engaging the government and the nation in warfare.
3. Comparative justice. War cannot be initiated justly unless the moral merit on the initiator's side clearly outweighs the moral merit on the other side. Because no state has absolute justice on its side, a sober answer must be given to the question: Is the justice of our cause greater than theirs?
4. Right intention. The intention for going to war must be morally right. War can be initiated only as a means to obtain genuine peace and reconciliation. The desire merely to punish or humiliate is not an adequate intention.
5. Last resort. All non-violent alternatives must be exhausted before resorting to war.
6. Probability of success. No war is justified if achievement of a successful end is clearly futile.
7. Proportionality of projected results. The good expected by resorting to war must be greater than the costs (estimated in the loss of human life and property) that may be foreseen as the result of the war.
8. Right spirit. War should not be engaged without an

attitude of regret that a just settlement could not be achieved any other way. War is always to be regarded as a tragic necessity.

(b) What are the principles for conducting a just war?

1. Proportionally in the use of force. The use of force should not exceed the nature of that aggression. No action should be generated that generates more harm than good.

2. Discrimination. A distinction must always be maintained between combatants and non-combatants. Although non-combatants may suffer or lose their lives as a result of military action, there must be no direct intention to take the lives of innocent civilians by attacking non-military targets.

3. Avoidance of evil means. There can be no use of evil means such as the execution of prisoners, the taking of hostages, pillaging, the threatening and violation of civilians, and the desecrating of holy places.

4. Good faith. The enemy must be treated with good faith in order to keep open the possibility of reconciliation once hostilities have ceased. Even enemies should be treated with human dignity.

The most important contrasting approach to the just war ethic is the "crusade." Sometimes called a "holy war" or "jihad," crusade treats war as an unconditional struggle of good against evil. The objective of a crusade is to destroy evil. Crusade often, if not always, assumes that some religious authority stands behind the effort; therefore, the underlying cause justifying crusade is considered "holy." In short, a crusade is waged by the authority of God in the name of some overriding ideal. As a consequence, there is no place for moral restraint; indeed, the conduct of war is thought to be above the law and not subject to moral codes because it is waged for God. There is, therefore, no distinction between combatant and non-combatant, for a crusade does not seek to restore some previous state, but to punish, conquer, and destroy. As for the morality of crusade, it is highly unlikely that there is a moral or Scriptural basis for a crusade, other than for one instigated by God Himself.

Was, then, the Civil War a just war, or was it a crusade? We can answer this question by examining in greater detail the principles of just war theory.

Just Cause

Conciliatory on the slave issue at first, Lincoln launched the war to keep the South in the Union. However, it is clear that the Southern Confederacy acted within its moral and constitutional rights in withdrawing from the Union. As we saw above, the South had the right to secede, and Lincoln had no constitutional right to prevent that from happening.

Competent Authority

The Constitution divides war powers between the Congress and the president. This division was intended by the framers to ensure that wars would not be entered into easily: it takes two keys, not one, to start the engine of war. This division of powers leaves the president with some exclusive powers as Commander-in-Chief (such as decisions on the field of battle), Congress with certain other exclusive powers (such as the ability to declare war and to appropriate dollars to support the war effort), and a sort of "twilight zone" of concurrent powers. In the zone of concurrent powers, the Congress might effectively limit presidential power, but in the absence of express congressional limitations the president is free to act.

In launching the war, Lincoln basically acted alone. In 1860, Lincoln's own Republican Party platform stated: "Resolved. That we, the delegated representatives of the Republican electors of the United States, in Convention assembled, in discharge of the duty we owe to our constituents and our country, unite in the following: That the maintenance inviolate of the rights of the States, and especially the right of each State to order and control its own domestic institutions according to its own judgment exclusively, is essential to that balance of powers on which the perfection and endurance of our political fabric depends, and we denounce the lawless invasion by armed force of the soil of any State or Territory, no matter under what pretext, as among the gravest of crimes."

Nevertheless, in the absence of congressional authority, Lincoln launched an attack against sovereign soil.

Comparative Justice

Did the moral merit of the North clearly outweigh that of the South? In his book *The Real Lincoln*,[15] Thomas DiLorenzo has pointed out that the Civil War was not fought over slavery. It was fought over money and politics. When Lincoln entered office his political agenda did not include ending slavery. Instead, he sought to create a strong, centralized government that would enable him to implement his long-held agenda of protective tariffs, centralized banking, and "internal improvements" (i.e., government subsidies to politically favored industries such as the railroad and canal-building companies that bankrolled the Republican Party). Lincoln was quite willing to let the South keep its slaves and to enforce the Fugitive Slave Law as long as the Southern states remained in the Union and continued to pay their disproportionate share of the taxes. Of course, Americans had long been divided into two camps, with the Hamiltonians favoring a highly centralized state, and the Jeffersonians favoring a more limited role for the federal government. However, it would be difficult to prove that the moral merit of the Hamiltonians clearly outweighed that of the Jeffersonians, or that America should have fought a war to decide the issue.

Right Intention

Here again, the right of secession and self-defense was the issue. The right of Southerners to defend themselves against the invasion of their duly constituted nation was recognized by foreign nations, especially Britain. The British press wrote, "It does seem the most monstrous of anomalies that a government founded on the 'sacred right of insurrection' should pretend to treat as traitors and rebels six or seven million people who withdrew from the Union, and merely asked to be left alone." Again, the British asked, "With what pretence of fairness can you Americans object to the secession of the Southern States when your nation was founded on secession from the British Empire?" Thus Charles Dickens concluded, "The Northern onslaught upon slavery was no more than a piece of specious humbug to conceal its desire for economic control of the Southern states."

Last Resort

Lincoln clearly ignored numerous appeals from both Northern and Southern statesmen for a non-violent solution to the division facing the nation. The South wanted no war, and Northern statesmen advised Lincoln: "Let our wayward sisters go." The promises of the Union Secretary of State that Fort Sumter would be turned over to South Carolina were twice-broken. Lincoln then called for 75,000 men to coerce the seven states of the Lower South back into the Union. Disregarding their own safety and security, the four states of the Upper South linked their destiny with the Confederacy, and the holocaust began.

America did not need a war to end slavery. Every other Western nation that held slaves in the nineteenth century—including Argentina, Brazil, Chile, Colombia, Ecuador, Jamaica, Mexico, Peru, Uruguay, and Venezuela—freed them peacefully. Most historians agree that the South would have done the same long before the end of the century. The fact that seven slave-holding states had seceded from the Union when Lincoln was elected would only have accelerated the process. Many people in the North considered the 1850 Fugitive Slave Act an abomination, and the law would almost certainly have been repealed had Lincoln allowed the Southern states to secede. Moreover, the Constitution of the Confederate

States of America prohibited the importation of slaves (Article I, Section 9), so that with their supply of slaves restricted, and with slaves now having a place to escape to, slavery in the Confederacy would have ended, as it did elsewhere, without war.

Probability of Success

On the basis of just war reasoning, putting soldiers in harm's way for a futile cause is never justified. Undoubtedly Lincoln believed that in waging war against the South the prospects for success were high. The North had over four times the population and over twenty times the industrial capacity of the South. During the war, Lincoln managed to get 100,000 immigrants from Europe to join the fight. Little did he know that victory would require an unprecedented loss of life. Before the Battle of Cold Harbor (June 3, 1864), for example, Grant's 50,000 Union soldiers had a premonition of death as they pinned their names on the backs of their uniforms. That day would see continuous waves of brave, blue-clad soldiers march to their deaths. Confederate General Evander Law would later say, "I had seen nothing to exceed this. It was not war, it was murder." Incredibly, Grant would order a second attack, having the same effect. President Lincoln remained silent at the White House, knowing that Grant could at least "face the numbers." Unlike Lee, Grant could afford the loss of so many men.

Proportionality of Projected Results

Lincoln's invasion of the South involved unbelievable costs. An official estimate of the financial cost of the war made in 1879 concluded that it totaled $6,190,000,000. Total military casualties were estimated at 623,026 dead. Total deaths, including civilian deaths from all causes, were estimated at 1,094,453. The Confederacy alone spent $2,099,808,707. By 1906 another $3.3 billion had already been spent by the U.S. government on Northerners' pensions and other benefits for former Federal soldiers.

Right Spirit

That the attitude of many Northern generals was vindictive and incompatible with just war theory is clear from many quotes attributed to them (see below).

Proportionally in the Use of Force

In the just war doctrine, "total war" is never warranted. Instead, the use of force must always be restrained and limited to that needed to reverse the unjust situation. Nevertheless, Lincoln replaced the rules of civilized warfare with the logic of "primitive warfare."

Discrimination

Lincoln's policy of waging war on civilian areas shocked European observers. Lincoln justified his policy on the grounds that he was dealing, not with a traditional war, but with a rebellion, in which the entire enemy population might be treated as criminals and traitors. Of course, even Lincoln was unable to apply this view consistently, for it would have meant executing nearly every Southerner, soldier or civilian.

As DiLorenzo and others have frequently pointed out, during the war Union commanders pillaged the South, abusing civilians in unspeakable ways, destroying railroads and factories, and burning private homes, public buildings, schools, and libraries. Union forces also slaughtered livestock and decimated crops, after they took what they wanted. As early as the first major battle of the war, the Battle of First Manassas in July of 1861, federal soldiers were plundering and burning private homes in the northern Virginia countryside. Such behavior quickly became so pervasive that on June 20, 1862, one year into the war, General McClellan, commanding the Army of the Potomac, wrote Lincoln a letter imploring him to see to it that the war was conducted according to "the highest principles known to Christian civilization" and to avoid targeting the civilian population to the extent that that was possible. Lincoln replaced McClellan a few months later and ignored his letter.

The Geneva Convention of 1863 condemned the bombardment of cities occupied by civilians, but Lincoln ignored all such restrictions on his behavior. The bombardment of Atlanta destroyed 90 percent of the city, after which the remaining civilian residents were forced to depopulate the city just as winter was approaching and the Georgia countryside had been stripped of food by the Federal army. In his memoirs, Sherman boasted that his army destroyed more than 100 million dollars in private property and carried home 20 million more during his famous "march to the sea."

After the Confederate army had finally evacuated the Shenandoah Valley in the autumn of 1864, Philip Sheridan's 35,000 infantry troops essentially burned the entire valley to the ground. As Sheridan described it in a letter to General Grant, in the first few days his soldiers "destroyed over 2200 barns... [and] over 70 mills [and] have driven in front of the army over 4000 head of stock, and have killed...not less than 3000 sheep.... Tomorrow I will continue the destruction."

Periodic reports detailing such carnage were sent to General Halleck in Washington, who shared them with President Lincoln. In a typical report issued on September 17, 1863, Union General Sherman made this comment: "We will remove every obstacle—if need be, take every life, every acre of land, every particle of property, everything that to us seems proper." Halleck showed this report to Lincoln, who enjoyed it so much that he demanded it be published. When Robert E. Lee invaded Pennsylvania in 1863, many Southerners hoped that he would give the Yankees a taste of their own medicine. But Lee was a man of integrity. Not only did he prohibit "wanton injury to private property," he also ordered his soldiers to pay for any supplies taken from civilians.

Avoidance of Evil Means

Lincoln consistently violated the rights of both civilians and Confederate prisoners of war. He suspended habeas corpus, and some 13,000 people were thrown into prison on charges that were never brought or made known. In his proclamation of September 24,

1864, Lincoln ordered that all citizens who engaged in "disloyal practices" would be tried in military tribunals, with such practices being decided by Lincoln himself. The Chief Justice of the Supreme Court, Roger B. Taney, informed Lincoln that he was violating the Constitution he had sworn an oath to uphold. Lincoln issued orders to arrest Taney but then thought better of assaulting the most respected man in the country.

Good Faith

Many examples could be given of the North's lack of good faith. Their vindictive spirit is seen in the fact that, after Lincoln's assassination, an illegal military tribunal convicted six innocent people and murdered four of them based on manufactured testimony known to be perjured when it was offered. Two of the three main government witnesses testified under false names because they were so disreputable, and one was later convicted of perjury in another case. The third was certified by the Canadian government as a fraud. A fourth witness, Louis Weichmann, had false testimony coerced out of him and later recanted, saying that Mrs. Mary Surratt was innocent. Surratt was the first woman executed by the United States.

Was, then, Lincoln's invasion of the South morally justified? In light of the tenets of just war theory discussed above, the answer is clearly no. Southerners were not fighting a war of rebellion against constitutional government. The states seceded so that they could *return* to constitutional government. The victory of the North represented the triumph of centralization over the principles of federalism, self-government, and liberty under the law.

After the so-called Emancipation Proclamation was issued, the war became a "crusade." By mid-war, the abolition of slavery had become the focal point of the war effort, which was now viewed as a holy cause. Nowhere is this more clearly seen than in Julia Ward Howe's *Battle Hymn of the Republic*, in which John Brown's "crusade" of liberating the slaves through insurrection and bloodshed is blasphemously made the equivalent of Jesus' death on the cross to save men from the slavery of sin.

In the end, it was this crusade mentality that justified in the minds of Northerners Sherman's idea of "total war." As he put it, "The entire South, man, woman, and child, is against us," adding that "We are not fighting against hostile armies, but a hostile people, and must make old and young, rich and poor, feel the hard hand of war." This intentional targeting of defenseless civilians was a war crime of sufficient proportion to condemn Lincoln's invasion of the South. Had the Confederates won the war, they undoubtedly would have been justified in bringing Lincoln and the entire Union command to trial for waging an immoral war against noncombatants.

Jefferson Davis, on April 7, 1861, said, "With the Lincoln administration rests the responsibility of precipitating a collision and the fearful evils of a cruel war." Many Northerners agreed. Benjamin J. Williams, a Massachusetts writer, said, "The South was invaded and a war of subjugation, destined to be the most gigantic which the world has ever seen, was begun by the Federal government against the seceding States, in complete and amazing disregard of the foundation principle of its own existence, as affirmed in the Declaration of Independence, that governments derive their just powers from the consent of the governed."

Ironically, it was Lincoln himself who said it best. In a speech to Congress on January 12, 1848, Lincoln declared:

> Any people, anywhere, being inclined and having the power, have the right to rise up and shake off the existing government, and form a new one that suits them better. This is a most valuable, a most sacred right—a right which we hope and believe is to liberate the world. Nor is this right confined to cases in which the whole people of an existing government may choose to exercise it. Any portion of such people, that

can, may revolutionize, and make their own of so much
of the territory as they inhabit.

Had Lincoln practiced what he preached, the bloodiest and most
unnecessary war in American history might well have been avoided.

— *Chapter 5* —

Not Guilty by Reason of Sanity: Why I Reject Government "Solutions" to Our Problems

"Isn't it the job of government to help all those people?" The question was being put to the governor of Oregon by a BBC reporter. That British network had been broadcasting a story about poverty in Oregon, where the unemployment rate is currently the highest in the nation at eight percent. Tax-strapped as are all the state chief executives, the governor replied that it was the fault of the *federal* government for not alleviating Oregon's plight.

Later in the report a parent in the hip Portland suburb of Beaverton was interviewed. It was back-to-school day, and the big story was the fact that parents in Beaverton had actually voted to *raise* their taxes to provide "much needed" services for their children. The parent in question said he had supported a tax increase so that the school would not lose its physical education funding— apparently an intolerable prospect for him.

This is a good illustration of the two views of America prevalent in our society today. On the one hand are those who hold to traditional, republican values of self-responsibility and freedom; on the other side are those who believe that Big Brother should solve all their problems. This clash over societal ideals has been around for a long time, and none of us is exempt from it.

A September 2003 edition of *Freedom Watch* noted that not a single one of the following taxes existed 100 years ago, when our nation had the largest middle class in the world and no national debt:

- Accounts Receivable Tax
- Building Permit Tax
- Capital Gains Tax
- Cigarette Tax
- Corporate Income Tax
- Court Fines
- Dog License Tax
- Federal Income Tax
- Federal Unemployment Tax
- Fishing License Tax
- Food License Tax
- Fuel Permit Tax
- Gasoline Tax
- Hunting License Tax
- Inheritance Tax Interest Expense
- Inventory Tax
- IRS Penalties
- Liquor Tax
- Local Income Tax
- Luxury Taxes
- Marriage License Tax
- Medicare Tax
- Property Tax
- Real Estate Tax
- Septic Permit Tax
- Service Charge Taxes
- Social Security Tax
- Road Usage Taxes

- Sales Taxes
- Recreational Vehicle Tax
- Road Toll Booth Taxes
- School Tax
- State Income Tax
- State Unemployment Tax
- Telephone Federal Excise Tax
- Telephone Federal Universal Service Fee Tax
- Telephone Federal, State, and Local Surcharge Taxes
- Telephone Minimum Usage Surcharge Tax
- Telephone Recurring and Non-Recurring Charges Tax
- Telephone State and Local Tax
- Telephone Usage Charge Tax
- Toll Bridge Taxes
- Toll Tunnel Taxes
- Traffic Fines (indirect taxation)
- Trailer Registration Tax
- Utility Taxes
- Vehicle License Registration Tax
- Vehicle Sales Tax
- Watercraft Registration Tax
- Well Permit Tax
- Workers Compensation Tax

It's obvious that freedom from oppressive government regulation is a thing of the past in America. The opportunity to compete in a free and open society is fast disappearing, and the "progressives" are doing all they can to hasten the complete demise of republicanism. Their idea of "liberty" is special status based on race, social disabilities, and personal and sexual preferences. And they have enormous muscle due to the support they receive from those in positions of power in society, big-spending Democrats and Republicans alike.

Radical social engineering has become the name of the game. In 1950 only two percent of the income of the average family of four went to pay taxes. Today, when state, local, and property taxes are included, the typical family of four spends about 47 percent of its income on taxes. Through our immoral and unconstitutional welfare system the government has kept people in poverty and has created a dependency that is virtually impossible to break. Thus, "Isn't it the job of the government to help all those people?" may well be *the* question of the day. If you believe the answer is no, if you want to join the growing band of freedom-lovers in America, then welcome to the most politically incorrect movement in history. But realize this: It will take a supreme effort by all of us to reverse the damage that the decades of socialism have done to the families of our nation.

The Scandal of the "Great Society"

The origin of the socialist welfare state in America is not difficult to trace. In his first State of the Union address on January 8, 1964, President Lyndon Baines Johnson announced: "This Administration today, here and now, declares unconditional war on poverty." On August 20 of the same year Johnson signed into law his first antipoverty bill—the Equal Opportunities Acts—declaring, "Today, for the first time in the history of the human race, a great nation is able to make and is willing to make a commitment to eradicate poverty among it people."

After defeating Republican candidate Barry Goldwater in the 1964 election, Johnson expanded his war on poverty themes in his January 4, 1965, State of the Union address. He requested federal funds to assist the elderly, the poor, black Americans, needy children, immigrants, and the mentally ill. He requested legislation to improve education, to provide scholarships and loans, to increase mental and physical health services, to raise Social Security benefits, to double the war against poverty, to improve the inner city, to provide housing, to fight crime and delinquency, and to protect the environment. Johnson proposed to use government to "keep our nation prosperous...to open opportunity to all our people...and to improve the quality of American life."

Each of these "Great Society" programs seemed absolutely necessary and worthwhile. But there were serious flaws lurking just below the surface. "It became an exercise in grantsmanship," said Jack Flynn of the Department of Housing and Urban Development. "In the end, those that got the money were the ones that wrote the best grant applications and had the best connections in Washington." The Great Society determined that the federal government could, on its own, eliminate poverty and transform the nation. It couldn't. The programs were top-heavy, benefiting staff more than the poor they were intended to assist. Top-heaviness grew until the federal government became the nation's top employer. The Community Action Program, for example, grew to employ more than 180,000 people in 907 different agencies that spent about $1.2 billion each year.

Just ten years after Johnson initiated his Great Society program, his successor Richard Nixon declared that much of its structure needed dismantling. Referring to the ambitious programs launched in the 1960s, he said, "The intention...was laudable. But the results, in case after case, amounted to dismal failure.... Too much money has been going to those who were supposed to help the needy and too little to the needy themselves." Though hundreds of billion of dollars were spent by the federal government to fund Great Society initiatives, millions of Americans still lived in poverty, the problem of nation illiteracy only increased, and adequate medical care was still beyond the reach of masses of Americans.

But the Great Society created by Lyndon Johnson left another kind of legacy as well. It bred a new sense of dependency on government to solve our troubles. President Johnson undoubtedly loved the country and wanted to help its people. He did his best to mobilize the federal government to solve the problems of the world. But he failed, and the nation has been saddled with the cost of that failure ever since. As James Antle[16] notes in an essay entitled, "Government Not the Solution to All Problems":

Notice the assumption that the choice is between government redistribution of wealth and the mass starvation of the poor. There can be no way to care for the poor without the government forcibly extracting compassion from people's paychecks. This does not take into consideration that perhaps a compassionate society's obligation to its unfortunate members belongs to families, communities and individuals, not government. Maybe there is more to compassion than simply endorsing new government programs and supporting politicians who promise to keep as many people as possible on the public dole.

The Great Society also explains why the public tends to support government growth. In contemporary America, the state has become a god, a super-problem solver, and if you don't support government solution to our problems you must be opposed to that problem being solved.

It's obvious that such spending is acceptable to President George W. Bush, who has been described oxymoronically as a "big government conservative" who joins tax relief to huge government programs. But here's what I want to know: How come people aren't asking if the president's new budget is worth it? Bush's 2004 federal budget would increase funds for community health centers from $169 million to $1.6 billion. It would include a $1.35 billion increase in the Federal Pell Grant program (for an all-time high of $12.7 billion) and $2.7 billion for conservation programs under the new farm bill. Under the president's proposal, museum programs would be funded at $34,430,000, while $41 billion would go to homeland security, including $890 million to develop new vaccines for smallpox, anthrax, and botulinum toxin. The president's budget even requests $288.2 million for weatherization, including $1.8 million for low-income families in New Hampshire. We could add to this $174 billion for crop insurance; $3.9 billion for the Puerto Rican

Nutrition Assistance Block Grant; $250 billion for Medicare; $177 billion for Medicaid; $38 billion for Housing and Urban Development (HUD); and $509 billion for the Social Security Administration. And the list goes on and on.

Meanwhile, the Congressional Budget Office projects deficits of $401 billion in 2003, $480 billion in 2004, and $1.5 trillion over the decade—figures that exclude the costs of Medicare drug benefits, extending expiring tax provisions, and reforming the Alternative Minimum Tax and that ignore the fact that discretionary spending, including defense spending, will likely grow faster than inflation. Factoring in those costs raises the projected annual deficits to between $600 billion and $700 billion through the coming decade.

Where does this ever-expanding national deficit come from? Certainly defense spending has played a role, but the real culprit is the largest domestic spending spree since the Great Society. According to Brian Riedl of the Heritage Foundation,[17] mandatory spending reached 11.1 percent of GDP in 2003, its highest level in history. In addition, non-defense discretionary spending in 2003 hit 3.9 percent of GDP for the first time since 1985. So are lawmakers talking about spending cuts? Hardly. The number of corporate welfare and pork projects has *doubled* since 2000, from everything from funding for education and health research to dozens of small, low-priority programs.

Does anybody seriously think that if the Founding Fathers came back and looked at all this domestic spending they would side with the Republican administration? It's time for a massive assault on the humanistic and bigoted Washington culture that wastes taxpayers' dollars on "freedom" and "compassion." Christians should be put to shame by the zealous activity of the liberal elite whose houses are built on sand while we, with our houses supposedly built on the rock, sit silently and look on. Using politics and what's left of the Constitution, we must stall the advance of welfare socialism and then, in the name of liberty, regain the ground we have lost.

We are now learning in America—or should be learning—that big government is like a huge monster with an insatiable appetite. The more it feeds, the more it grows in its ever-increasing lust.

Call Out the Obesity Police

If you need more proof of the ability of government to squander the largess of its people, consider the case of the fat police. They've been called the obesity police, food nags, health nannies, and nut cases. And those are the polite terms. They are the people behind the recent campaign to make purveyors of junk food the next Big Tobacco, suing over the products' effects on health. All of this is completely laughable, of course, unless you are a restaurant owner and have already lost business due to smoking bans and can't imagine how you can afford to fight the government on the food issue. A lawyer appearing on Fox's *Hannity and Colmes* argued that since obesity costs society billions of dollars in medical costs, businesses that provide unhealthy food should be liable. Both the conservative and liberal hosts tried to make a case for personal responsibility, but the lawyer still insisted that Ronald McDonald should be held accountable for the girth of the nation.

While there's no disputing that obesity has risen dramatically in the last decade or so (especially among children), so has fake fatness. In 1998, the government changed the formula for how fatness is measured and, all of a sudden, another 30 million Americans woke up fat when they had gone to bed skinny. But if you really want to see excess fat, take a look at the potbellied government bureaucrats who are supposedly charged with spending our tax dollars in a fiscally responsible manner. Despite a weak congressional effort to stem government waste, the misuse of taxpayers' money continues unabated. The following list is merely a sampling of the problems within executive branch departments and agencies.

• A government grant pays women as much as $75 to watch pornographic videos. You heard me right. The U.S. government is paying 180 lesbian, bisexual, and heterosexual women to watch "erotic video clips of lesbian, gay or heterosexual interactions" to assess their arousal response to pornography. The study, being conducted at Northwestern University, claims that measuring a woman's response to pornography will help us understand the "phenomenology of sexual orientation," whatever *that* means.

• In an effort to improve foreign aid, President Bush has proposed a new program, the Millennium Challenge Account, which will cost $5 billion annually by fiscal 2006 and will "complement" existing foreign aid programs. In other words, the agency will add to taxpayers' ever-growing burden. The U.S. is already the world leader in humanitarian assistance and food aid, providing more than $2.5 billion globally in fiscal 2001. It is also the top provider of Official Development Assistance, with $11 billion in fiscal 2001. The stated goal of the Millennium Challenge is to increase assistance to certain developing countries by 50 percent over three years.

• The Department of Agriculture has made $1.3 billion in erroneous payments in its Food Stamp program. Cheaters collect more than their fair share of food stamps by misrepresenting their income, failing to report deceased food stamp receivers, and using false identification to register more than once for benefits. In 1996 alone, food stamp fraud was $5 billion out of the then-$27 billion program. In addition, the department's Rural Utility Service continues to have problems with its electricity loan program. The RUS is in the process of writing off $3 billion of a total $4.1 billion in loans owed by one borrower, which has been in bankruptcy since December 1994. Between 1992 and 1997, the RUS wrote off debts totaling almost $2 billion for electricity loan borrowers.

• The Environmental Protection Agency has been unsuccessful in recovering its costs from responsible parties under the Superfund hazardous waste cleanup program. At the end of fiscal year 1998, EPA had agreements to recover only $2.4 billion of about $11 billion it had spent on the Superfund program.

• The Department of Energy estimates that its National Ignition Facility at the Lawrence Livermore National Laboratory in California will cost over $1 billion more than originally planned. Unresolved technical problems may further drive up the cost of the facility.

• A Federal land exchange program designed by the Department of the Interior to protect wildlife habitat and enhance recreational areas has shortchanged taxpayers by millions of dollars. The department's Bureau of Land Management and the Department of Agriculture's Forest Service failed to ensure that land being exchanged was appropriately valued or that exchanges served the public interest. In one instance a private buyer acquired 70 acres of Federal land for $763,000, and sold the parcel the same day for $4.6 million. The same buyer acquired another 40 acres at a value of $504,000 and sold the land the same day for $1 million.

These examples illustrate just how much mismanagement of our hard-earned money takes place in the departments and agencies of the federal government. Our politicians spend first, and then ask how to pay for it (maybe), and then waste what they don't even have. There aren't many families that buy a house first and then determine whether or not they can afford it, but Congress plays by its own rules.

The Best Welfare Reform

As of this writing, Congress is about to vote on whether to continue the historic welfare reform legislation adopted in 1996. Rejecting the traditional notion of individual and community responsibility for oneself and one's neighbor, the Bush administration is promoting a $17 billion cash assistance package for the states. According to the Cato Institute,[18] while the president claims this package will "hold the line" on spending, it actually is a $500 million increase from the current congressional appropriation of $16.5 billion and nearly $4 billion more than actual spending by the states. The report also states that "the president wants to promote marriage among single welfare mothers ... [and] will press for $300 million in spending on programs to resolve marital conflicts, improve marital communications, reduce the divorce rate, and address problems of alcoholism, infidelity, and gambling that negatively affect families."

The truth is that neither the Democrats nor the Republicans have a workable—let alone biblical or constitutional—model for welfare reform. The Democrats want to "end welfare as we know it" by spending more money on failed government jobs, education, and health programs. The Republicans want to "end welfare as we know it" by funneling money through the hands of Washington and then back to the states so they can spend it on the same failed welfare programs. The bottom line is that not one wasteful program will be eliminated. Both approaches are based on flawed political and economic assumptions. They assume that the federal government has legal authority to create or administer a welfare program. As we have seen, however, Congress has only those powers that are explicitly granted to it by the U.S. Constitution. I believe that any person who will read the Constitution with an unbiased mind will conclude that if our Constitution is to have any meaning at all there is absolutely no federal authority for welfare programs.

I am astounded by the Bush administration's bald assertion regarding the capabilities of the federal government to transform human life, including marriage. The state has taken over the role of God! Government employs us, feeds us, regulates us, and now claims to be able to solve our problems, including gambling (is Bill Bennett listening?). For many Americans, the state has become their church, and the federal government has become an idol, stripping individuals and communities of their social responsibilities and engaging in the immoral transfer of wealth. And since the New Deal, a trickle has become a flood.

To no one's surprise, Bush's proposal provides no systematic justification for involving government in welfare. The reason is obvious. There can be no justification given for the state usurping the function of private individuals and the church. I agree with Congressman Ron Paul[19] that "the federal welfare state is neither moral nor constitutional." The tragedy is that America has become a secular nation populated by a majority that rejects the Lordship of Jesus Christ. Christianity has allied itself with the governments of the day, while the transcendent gospel has become submerged in the world's values.

The Bible teaches that the *church* is to fulfill Paul's injunction to "do good to all men" by helping non-Christians in need—feeding the hungry, clothing the naked, housing the homeless, healing the sick. No believer is exempt from this responsibility (see Luke 3:11; 1 John 3:17; James 1:27). On the other hand, no Scripture supports an active government role in alleviating poverty or the use of coercive measures. Even Paul refused to command believers to help their less fortunate brothers, stating: "Each man should give what he has determined in his heart to give, not reluctantly or under compulsion, for God loves a cheerful giver" (2 Corinthians 9:7).

I realize that it is impolitic today to criticize the sacred cow of the "Great Society" and the "Welfare State." Merely to question the legitimacy of welfare is to commit blasphemy against the state. Nevertheless, I believe it is time for Christians to reject the gods of statism and socialism, including the misnamed "welfare" system. Government welfare is nothing more than poverty insurance. The welfare system has created endless incentives for teenage pregnancy and family breakups. And the state's remedy has become worse than the ailment. Writes Murray Rothbard in his *Man, Economy, and State*:[20]

> State poor relief is clearly a subsidization of poverty, for men are now automatically entitled to money from the state because of their poverty. Hence, the marginal

disutility of income foregone from leisure diminishes, and idleness and poverty tend to increase further, which in turn increases the amount of subsidy that must be extracted from the taxpayers. Thus, a system of legally subsidized poverty tends to call forth more of the very poverty that is supposedly being alleviated. A man will not work if he is assured of minimal comforts not working. The reason to work is simply not there as a man today can be paid by the government not to work.

In his book *Savior or Servant? Putting Government In Its Place*,[21] David Hall concludes: "Citizens of any age will do well to put the government in its proper place. The state is not to become Messianic nor play the role of Savior. It must thus be restrained from assuming duties or domains that God has not entrusted to it. Those things that God has prohibited the state from superintending must be kept from it."

Clearly it's not enough to reform the welfare system; it must be abolished. The answer to poverty is still to be found in individual benevolence exercised either privately or through the church, with the family as the first rung of relief. Meanwhile, Christians must continue to develop a systematic and intellectually rigorous definition of proper government action based on sound biblical principles and political theory, rather than on sentimentality or a vague sense of "justice."

If Liberty Mattered, We Wouldn't Even be Talking About School Vouchers

Compassionate conservatives are exuberant in their support of yet another Big Brother attempt to "fix" the public education fiasco in America—a voucher program for low-income families. While I'm not surprised that the idea of school vouchers has the backing of Bush and his colleagues, who eagerly latch on to every conceivable government solution to problems like lousy classroom instruction, I think my conservative friends are making a big mistake to go with big government on this issue just because it's politically expedient.

The philosophical problem of big government is not a side show in the circus we call the federal bureaucracy; it's the main event. If you as a parent feel your child is trapped in an under-performing government school, I can guarantee you that a government-sponsored voucher system will only add to your woes. Never forget Black's first rule of government: *Every dollar of federal funding has a sizeable string attached to it*. With vouchers, of course, the strands that are affixed are more subtle than with the typical government-sponsored "solution." But once the government's fingers touch the dough, it can and will insist that its own "standards"—as interpreted by its own educational bureaucrats—be followed.

To put this another way, federal money *for* education means federal control *of* education. Is it so hard to see this? If you still don't believe me, may I ask you to go to The Alliance for the Separation of School and State website[22] run by Marshall Fritz? Fritz shows clearly that school vouchers will only serve to change the culture of private schools to be public school look-alikes. Eventually, he argues, it will be impossible to send your children to religion-based schools at all. Are tax credits, then, the solution? Again, Marshall Fritz has the answer: "Some think tax credits are better than vouchers, but ultimately they are only camouflaged vouchers. Charter schools are just public schools on a longer leash. A dog on a leash is still a dog on a leash."

As always in American politics, the real issue boils down to traditional values such as freedom and self-responsibility. For me, the puzzler in all this discussion about vouchers is why conservative Christian leaders are celebrating government coercion when they should be pointing to the wisdom of Fritz's position. Conservatives must see that good education will never be based on government taking taxes paid by hardworking people and giving it to poor parents who will thus be enabled to leave public schools they weren't paying for in the first place. I also want to know this: When will Christian parents realize that the best and easiest way to avoid the tyranny of government education is by removing their children from the public schools altogether?

It's Time to Abolish Art Welfare

No less problematic than our mediocre public school system is our government's continued support for the National Endowment for the Arts (NEA)—one of the many driving forces that channel humanistic political and religious beliefs into the minds of the vast majority of Americans. The creation of the NEA by Johnson in 1965 was the culmination of unprecedented ties between American abstract artists and a federal government that celebrated them as visionaries and saw their output as a humanistic propaganda tool.

For example, in the late 1990s the NEA contributed $500,000 to help fund the Brooklyn Museum of Art's exhibit called "Sensation," which included a picture of the Virgin Mary covered with elephant feces, a picture of the Last Supper with a naked woman in the role of Christ, and a sculpture of a man's head filled with frozen blood. A New York film distributor once received $112,700 for producing films with explicitly lesbian sex scenes and sadomasochistic violence. The NEA has also supported Robert Mapplethorpe's homoerotic photography. And the list goes on and on. According to *Christianity Today*,[23] in May of 1997 the Christian Action Network displayed 40 NEA works on the Capitol steps as part of a traveling exhibit entitled, "A Graphic Picture Is Worth a Thousand Votes." Capitol police confiscated 17 pieces of art on the basis of obscenity.

Consider the irony of the situation. If an Alabama Supreme Court Chief Justice wants to display a monument containing the Ten

Commandments in the judicial building of his state, anti-religious pressure groups invoke the First Amendment to prosecute him for "unconstitutional" religious expression. But when people desecrate the nation's most sacred religious symbols, it is not only defended as "art" and "free speech" but we are asked to pay for it! After the Republicans took over Congress in 1994 we were told they would cut government down to size, and that the NEA was at the top of their list. Every year there's a budget battle over the funding of the NEA, and every year the NEA lobby wins. Like all public agencies, the first priority of the NEA is the preservation and expansion of its own budget.

Americans cannot afford to waste one more penny defending the National Endowment for the Arts. Art existed before 1965, and art will continue to thrive in America without federal funding. Admission tickets and private funding can more than compensate for pulling the plug on the unconditional subsidies provided by the NEA. Already corporations and private foundations contribute more than $9 billion annually to the arts. It's time to ask our politicians in Washington to take a stand: Will you or will you not continue to support federal subsidies for degenerate "art"? Do you or do you not agree that the NEA is beyond reform and should be abolished? Just as importantly, we have to ask ourselves: Am I willing to continue to support a political party that promises reform but consistently goes back on its word through compromise and inaction?

If parents want the best education for their children, let them stop sending them to those atheistic indoctrination centers we call public schools. And if businessmen want freedom from excessive taxation, let them oppose the spending policies government has used to impose an onerous tax burden that has forced wives and mothers into the workplace to relieve the financial burden laid on the family. The bottom line is that all of us must do more to restrain the government, to restrain the courts, and, most of all, to restrain ourselves.

Here again, the church must take a stand. We will not be able to do this until we are willing to stop diffusing our resources on pseudoproblems—card playing, dancing, smoking, and the like—

and begin concentrating again on matters of deep and significant morality involving state-sponsored theft and Edenic-style utopianism. What is needed is an evangelical community that is not itself such a supporter of big government that it aids and abets the country's problems instead of solving them. National revival is a possibility at any time, and the essential precondition for it is the reintroduction of the Word of God into all spheres of national life, including government.

— *Chapter 6* —

Brand New American Schools? No Thanks

> *For over one hundred years Americans have been running a gigantic experiment in government schools, trying to find out what a society looks like without God. Now we know.*
>
> — Douglas Wilson

In case you haven't noticed, a new generation of school "reformers" is viewing our school-aged children as so much human capital—raw material to be molded and shaped into the building materials for a New World Order. If you don't believe me, just try asking your local high school student to name his or her two Senators in Congress, or to quote the First Amendment, or to discuss states rights.

I know I'm reopening a can of worms, but I think the state of education in America today is tragic. Instead of teaching the next generation the core knowledge necessary to produce free, intelligent, and independent thinkers, our current educational efforts are directed toward creating a compliant, task-oriented workforce with politically correct beliefs and behavior. It's so easy to forget that the

U.S. Constitution doesn't even mention the issue of education for children. In fact, it leaves this matter entirely in the hands of the parents, where it belongs.

Just over a decade ago Lamar Alexander, while president of the University of Tennessee, gave a speech in which he challenged America's top educators to create what he called "brand new American schools." He said:

> I would think the brand new American school would be open year round—open from 6 a.m. until 6 p.m. A second characterization might be that these schools would serve children from age three months to eighteen years of age. A shocking thought to you—but if you were to do an inventory of every baby in your community and think about the needs of those babies for the next four or five years, you might see that those needs might not be served in any other way—they have to be served in some way—and maybe around the school. Or if you study a little more, you might go back to thinking the school might need to serve the pregnant mother of the baby in terms of prenatal care.

After making this amazing speech, Alexander was named U.S. Secretary of Education by then-President George H. W. Bush! Since that time we have seen control over education and employment practices move from individuals, families, local and state school boards, and state legislators to the unelected National Skills Standard and State Workforce Development Boards. Former President Clinton's plans for a national workforce of skilled laborers has been achieved through the Goals 2000 Educate America Act (HR 1804), the School-to-Work Opportunities Act (HR 2884), and the Improving America's School Act (HR 6). Our schools have been restructured to teach labor skills and to focus on changing attitudes and especially "unacceptable" social behaviors.

I simply cannot believe that responsible adults would ever want their children's education to be more about transferring phone calls than about the basic facts of American history, literature, science, and morality. Alas, therein lies the rub. Get into a political discussion with your peers these days and you will see what I mean.

"You mean to tell me that Bush has appointed homosexual activists to his administration?"

"Yes, that's right."

"But he's a born-again Christian!"

"I know, but he has promoted the gay agenda as much as any other president in history."

"I don't believe it."

"Well, when the man who occupies the White House puts homosexual activists at the table in his administration, promotes and signs pro-gay legislation, and refuses to meet with ex-gays and other Christian organizations to discuss the issue, doesn't it send a confusing message about his claim to be pro-family?"

"But he promised to restore honor to the White House during his presidential campaign, didn't he?"

"That's my point!"

The Tragedy of Secular Education

You may be saying to yourself, "But *my* child's school is an exception." Friends, after 30 years of federal "aid" to education, the ugly tentacles of the federal government now reach into every school district in the nation. The reality is that biblical principles are *banned* in your local public school and Jesus Christ is *robbed* of His deserved preeminence "in all things." The fact that state education is compulsory in America is no argument that it is legitimate. Indeed, the church must be extremely jealous of any attempt on the part of the state to take control of any aspect of the work of religious education.

Yet that is just what is happening in America. The entire weight of state-controlled education is molding the child to believe that the church and its message are unessential to the complete or normal life of an American citizen. No academic skepticism, no secularistic authors, no blatant materialism can so undermine the spiritual life of the country like the completely secularized training of the child under the authority of the state.

State schools dare not teach the spirit of the Constitution as set forth in the Declaration of Independence. They dare not teach it because it says that all men, not just the majority, are endowed by their Creator with unalienable rights, among which are life, liberty, and the pursuit of happiness. Again, state schools dare not teach that to secure these rights governments are instituted among men, deriving their just power from the consent of the governed. Instead, they teach the outmoded philosophy of the divine right of kings, only now they call it the divine right of the majority. State schools have to completely repudiate the ideals of the American way of life. They dare not teach the meaning of liberty. They dare not teach the meaning of the Golden Rule. They dare not teach youth that the ideal form of government—the only form of government that can be of value to mankind—is one that is limits the power of politicians by the "chains of the Constitution," as Thomas Jefferson once put it.

The best solution to America's education fiasco is to get the federal government out of our classrooms entirely, to repeal all federal meddling, and to let local communities and parents educate their children as they see fit. When the weight of the state is thrown against the Christian faith, the state has become the enemy of the faith and disaster lies ahead. The state, for the sake of its own legitimate functions, must recognize that national life is not conserved but destroyed if the policy of the state as a wholly secularized mode of education is to undermine the authority of the church.

American Education and the Constitution

This will come as a surprise to some people, but in the Constitution's careful enumeration of its powers and responsibilities (Article 1, Section 8) there is no mention of "education." This *laissez faire* attitude toward education by our Founding Fathers was not accidental. From at least the 1700s, common law has held that parents had total and complete authority over their children. This position has been steadfastly upheld by American courts for the past 200 years. This means that if homeschooling isn't considered equal to "private education" in a state's law, that law is unconstitutional. States may try and prove that they have "compelling interests" in controlling the education of children, but such a claim is a false boast. No one possesses a higher compelling interest in the education of their child than his or her parents. It is not only their right as parents, it is their responsibility.

The right of parents to control the education of their own children is protected by the Constitution under (1) freedom of speech, (2) freedom of religion, and (3) the right to privacy. But even more importantly, the right to educate our own children is a God-given, unalienable right. The U.S. Constitution doesn't give it to us; the federal government doesn't give it to us. God Himself has given it to us.

Thus the decision to withdraw from the public school system should be based not on what may be wrong in a public school but on a recognition that a God-centered and Bible-based education is mandatory for Christian parents. If you think you can keep your children in a secular school system and escape the dumbed-down, amoral, and immoral results of secular humanism in schools, you are sorely mistaken. The reason is that secular humanism is itself a religion. In fact, the biblical view of man's nature is in sharp conflict with secular humanism, which teaches that man is basically good. Every man-centered system of education is, consciously or unconsciously, built on this philosophy. Christians, on the other hand, speak of the "bondage of the will" (Luther) or "total depravity" (Calvin). The humanist believes that the evil a man does is the result of evil influences in his environment, but Jesus says that a man needs to get a new spiritual nature "from above" by being born again spiritually (John 3:3).

Some have argued that vouchers would bring better accountability by making all schools part of the public system. Vouchers may sound like the solution, but there are two unavoidable pitfalls: (1) federal school choice vouchers would only continue the unconstitutional federal involvement in education, and (2) government control always follows government money—if not immediately, most certainly eventually. In his fictional look at the future, *Brave New World*, written in 1934, Aldous Huxley wrote:

> A really efficient totalitarian state would be one in which the all-powerful executive of political bosses and their army of managers control a population of slaves who do not have to be coerced, because they love their servitude. To make them love it is the task assigned, in present-day totalitarian states, to the ministries of propaganda, newspaper editors *and school teachers* (emphasis added).

The "new" education imposed on America's schools in the last 60 years or so has fulfilled this prophecy almost to a "t." It's an education that has eroded and destroyed the biblical and constitutional foundations upon which a stable society must rest. In 1962, the U.S. Supreme Court banned Bible reading and a 22-word prayer recited in the schools of New York. The prayer the Supreme Court declared "unconstitutional" said:

> Almighty God, we acknowledge our dependence upon
> Thee, and we beg Thy blessings upon us, our parents,
> our teachers, and our Country.

If the Bible-based foundational concepts of education upon which our nation was built had not already been so badly eroded, there would have been a massive uprising of indignant parents in America. They would never have tolerated the Supreme Court's decision striking down what had been fully constitutional for 175 years. But because most Americans had already given up Bible reading and prayer in their own homes, they meekly accepted the court's appalling reinterpretation of law.

Let it be repeated: Our Founders did not give us our rights and freedoms. We didn't get them through our Bill of Rights or our Constitution. What makes America unique in the annals of history is that our Founding Fathers discovered and set forth the truth that the rights of the individual come not from a king, a government, or a Constitution, but from God. The Declaration of Independence affirms:

> We hold these truths to be self-evident, that all men are
> created equal, that they are endowed by their Creator
> with certain unalienable rights, that among these are
> Life, Liberty and the pursuit of Happiness. — That to
> secure these rights, Governments are instituted among
> Men, deriving their just powers from the consent of the
> governed.

If God Himself gives men their rights, then government can't tamper with them, and this includes the right of parents to control every aspect of their children's education.

Considering the Options

Two leaders in the movement to restore parental control to education are Marshall Fritz of the Alliance for the Separation of School and State and Rev. Ray Moore of the Exodus Mandate. Rev. Moore has written a manifesto entitled *Let My Children Go*, which is essential reading for parents who still operate under the illusion that our public schools are salvageable. In fact, according to Moore the phrase "public school" is a misnomer since the term implies that these schools serve and are answerable to the public. Far from it, he says. They answer to government bureaucrats, pure and simple. If you want schools that truly serve the public, try private or Christian schools that operate independently of Uncle Sam, he says.

Both Fritz and Moore have reached the same conclusion: Public schools are beyond reform and redemption. It costs American tax payers half a trillion dollars a year to teach young people to read and write. And the result? In Massachusetts, 60 percent of college graduates flunk the teacher-qualification exam. Most of those taking the exam are products of compulsory government education. After 150 years of tax-financed schooling, we see more and more children failing to grow into responsible, caring, competent adults. This is not to deny that there are some good teachers who are trying to make a difference. But as I see it, that's precisely the problem. The people in the public school system who have the least influence are the teachers themselves. The system has been strangled by laws, rules, and court orders that have paralyzed teachers and local administrators into inaction. Their reasoning is, "Why should I risk a lawsuit or being fired by rocking the boat?"

What, then, can parents do?

First, we must recognize that public schools are not value-neutral. They never have been. Government education is an intentional (and highly effective) effort by anti-theists to lead children away from their parents and from the church. That the prevailing philosophies and methodologies of American public education are leftist is not up for debate. Leftists have dominated the federal Department of Education, most state Departments of Education, the teachers' unions, and many teachers colleges and education foundations for decades. Most rank-and-file teachers know this, but the situation is so deplorable that they dare not speak out. Moreover, government schools have become killing grounds, especially for Christian children. Both the Columbine murders and those that occurred in West Paducah, Kentucky, are evidence that Christian students are prime targets of violence.

Second, we can consider sending our children to a private Christian school. Dr. D. James Kennedy of Coral Ridge Ministries has long championed Christian schools as alternatives to the public school system. The problem here, of course, is defining what "Christian" means. Just baptizing a secular educational approach with Christian terms doesn't guarantee that a truly biblical worldview is being taught. The two years I had my sons in a private Christian school only reaffirmed for me the problems inherent in all educational environments in terms of negative socialization. Cuss words, disrespectful attitudes, bullying, defiance toward authority— all these seeds of rebellion began to be planted in this private "Christian" school.

This leaves parents with one last option: homeschooling. Please do not dismiss this option out of hand. I can think of at least six good reasons to homeschool:

• God intended parents to be the primary educators of their children. We simply cannot trust the government to educate them for us; neither should we let the government take them from us.

• The family suffers when children are not educated at home. The way to destroy the family is by separating children from their parents. Government schools are constantly coming up with ways of undermining parental authority and bypassing parental responsibility.

• Homeschooled children do better academically. No doubt about it—the smaller the student-to-teacher ratio, the better the academic product. In fact, studies have shown that the longer a child is homeschooled, the significantly higher are his or her scores on standardized tests.

• Homeschooling produces the best socialization. Positive socialization does not come from spending twelve years with one's same age group, but from growing up in a loving and disciplined environment under the nurture of one's parents. Once again, the studies are in: Homeschooled children show higher levels in adaptability, social adjustment, and maturity while exhibiting lower levels in aggressive behavior, loudness, and competitiveness. Homeschoolers are more independently minded and more family oriented. They are less peer dependent, and much less government dependent.

• Homeschooling rises above the common morals of our society and produces the best values. Homeschooled children respect peers, parents, elders, and authorities; and they don't join gangs.

• Homeschooling helps us as parents, too. We never learn anything so well as when we teach it ourselves. By homeschooling we can finally master the math we never learned in school, the foreign language we always wanted to speak, the history we were never taught, or the science we learned from a completely secular point of view.

Homeschooling is, indeed, an excellent option. In fact, for more than three full lifetimes—the 220 years from the 1620s to the 1840s—American schooling was independent of government control, subsidy, and influence. From this educational freedom the American republic was born.

I know some of you are thinking, "We don't have enough time or money to homeschool, and even if we did we don't feel adequate to teach our own kids." The fact is: You *do* have enough time and money (if you are willing to make home education a priority) and you *can* teach effectively (there are hundreds of resources available today that will help you do that). If you are struggling with these questions and want some helpful advice, I recommend Lewis Goldberg's "The Time for Secession Has Come (...from the Public Schools, that is)."[24] His suggestions are extremely practical and are sufficient, I believe, to convince even the most skeptical parent that homeschooling is not only possible but also the best alternative to sending their children to government indoctrination centers or even private "Christian" schools.

Meanwhile, don't be fooled by the government's mantra, "Give us more money and we will do the job." Unless you see the federal Department of Education abolished, you will know the reforms are a sham.

— Chapter 7 —

Give Some People an Inch and They'll Think They're a Ruler: Neocon Foreign Policy and the Invasion of Iraq

Few things in current politics make me more frustrated or angry than seeing the statist "bait and switch" argument used by Washington politicians to justify our recent war with Iraq. The Bush administration, following its new "National Security Strategy" asserting that the U.S. will maintain global hegemony permanently, had led us into an unnecessary war that has cost the lives of thousands of Iraqis and hundreds of Americans. No weapons of mass destruction (WMD) have been found; no "imminent" threat to American security has been proved; acts of terrorism have increased; the ranks of al Qaeda have swollen; and the U.S. has become involved in a Vietnam-like quagmire from which it will take years to extract itself and which will almost certainly lead to a fiscal train wreck. The neoconservative elite in Washington tell us the U.S. is only "protecting" its own interests. What is being protected is U.S. power carried out unilaterally by America, reiterating the maxim of the Greek historian Thucydides that "large nations do what they wish, while small nations accept what they must."

Our unprovoked war of aggression against Iraq has done nothing but increase the anger and hatred of our enemies in the Middle East, whose motivation stemmed largely from our stationing of troops on holy ground in Saudi Arabia and from a brutal 12-year embargo of Iraq that contributed directly to the deaths of hundreds of thousands of innocent Iraqi civilians. The irony of this is not lost on the Iraqis. They recall that throughout the 70s the U.S. government was an ardent support of Saddam Hussein and even supplied him with WMD that he used against his own people, with the full knowledge of U.S. officials. Thus it was our own foreign policy, combined with our gross negligence to anticipate the attacks of 9/11 or to defend our porous borders, that engendered the terrorist attacks in New York and the Pentagon.

Meanwhile, the bellocrats are trying their best to persuade a gullible and confiding American public that an unconstitutional war in Iraq was in our best interests. Yet they have begun to suffer defeats in the light of world opposition, including opposition from American allies who refuse to be bluffed by the Jabberwocky being emitted *ad nauseum* from the War Room. In his essay entitled "The Iraq Dilemma: An Illegitimate Occupation,"[25] George Hunsinger concluded:

> Everything that antiwar critics said about Iraq has turned out to be true. Before the invasion they voiced their concerns that Iraq posed no imminent threat to the United States, that it was not directly linked to the war on terrorism, that an invasion might make the terrorism problem worse, that there was no international coalition supporting the war, and that there were other ways to contain Saddam Hussein. Now the United States, with no real allies inside the country, has months, not years, before it is forced out in defeat, if it

persists down its current path. The situation could unravel into chaos at any time. Above all, every death in this war is unnecessary, because the war was unnecessary.

Instead of answering their critics' objections in an intellectually honest way, the administration's minions bask in their sense of righteous indignation against an evil regime that was felt to be a threat by practically no one in Europe and the Middle East, its closest neighbors included. The disinformation continues unabated, with no intermezzo in sight, the administration undoubtedly counting on continued support for its Iraqi policy from the hoi polloi now that the war is in occupation mode. Everyone but the president and his cabinet seems to realize that this disastrous foreign policy will put an end to whatever credibility America once had in the Middle East and among our ever-more estranged and alienated European allies.

Recently Chuck Baldwin[26] wondered aloud whether America was the revived Holy Roman Empire. Sometimes I wonder the same thing. How much longer can the neocon spinmeisters get away with redefining the American vision? When will we be able to have a genuine debate in this country on the singular issue facing Americans today: the question of whether these United States will remain a republic as envisioned by our Founders or will degenerate into a global empire? The anger of the populace is not far below the surface, and it will take more than the chest-thumping of the bellocrats to squelch the thunder.

The Arrogance of Power

For me, at least, our leaders' cozenage is but another reminder that the Christian's real warfare is "against the principalities, against the powers, against the world rulers of this present darkness, against the spiritual hosts of wickedness" (Ephesians 6:12). It gives me no pleasure to say it, but it appears that our president has thrown all semblance of humility out the window. Hubris is the watchword of the day. Hubris is one of those wonderful Greek words that captures a thought better than any English counterpart ever could. According to the *American Heritage Dictionary of the English Language*, it means: "Overbearing pride or presumption; arrogance," even "wanton violence." While I could cite numerous examples of the president's hubris, I will mention only three.

The first is his dismissive attitude vis-à-vis the international community which, despite the administration's vigorous efforts to convince it otherwise, continues to raise serious questions about our military operation in Iraq in terms of its legality, its justification, its political implications, and its costs both militarily and politically. Even the British Parliament has revolted against Prime Minister Tony Blair, telling him that the case for war and occupation has never been made, according to the *Guardian Unlimited*.[27] Is the empire worth it? Our allies say no.

Prior to the war, Iraq was in violation of UN Security Council Resolution 687 (in addition to a number of subsequent resolutions relating to it). This resolution required full cooperation with UN inspectors ensuring that Iraq's WMD were destroyed. However, the Security Council did not specify military enforcement mechanisms in Resolution 687, nor did it do so in any of its subsequent resolutions. Although the Security Council warned Iraq that noncompliance would have "severest consequences" (Resolution 1154), it declared that it alone had the authority to "ensure implementation of this resolution and peace and security in the area."

President Bush was aware that Articles 41 and 42 of the UN Charter declare that no member state has the right to enforce any resolution militarily unless the UN Security Council has determined that there has been a material breach of its resolution and decides that all nonmilitary means of enforcement have been exhausted. At that point—and only at that point—can the Security Council specifically authorize the use of military force, which is precisely what it did in November 1900 with Resolution 678 in response to Iraq's invasion of Kuwait. The fact that the UN took no such step with respect to Iraq made no difference to Bush. Moreover, not one of Iraq's neighbors had called on the United States to help it defend itself. This is because none of them felt threatened by Saddam Hussein. Bush seems to little think—and care even less—that the world community views the U.S. and not Iraq as the aggressor nation in current conflict, in contrast to the Persian Gulf War of 1990-91. Am I the only one that sees a small contradiction here?

Secondly, and even more disturbing to me, was the president's refusal to submit his case against Iraq to the Congress of the United States, which alone is constitutionally empowered to issue a declaration of war. Article 1, Section 8, of the U.S. Constitution states that "The Congress shall have power...To declare war...." Here the language is simple, intentionally so. Our Founding Fathers insisted that the decision to go to war was to be made by the legislative branch of government, and not by the executive. The reasoning of the Founders was simple: it is far too dangerous to place the power to wage war in the hands of a single individual.

The October 2002 resolution passed by Congress is often cited as proof that the president had congressional authority to attack Iraq. Nothing could be further from the truth. The resolution declared war against no nation but simply stated that the president "has authority under the Constitution to take action in order to deter and prevent acts of international terrorism against the United States...." The resolution by Congress could not, in fact, grant the president authority to declare war because the Congress cannot alter the express language of the Constitution. Only a constitutional amendment can overrule Article 1, Section 8. For these reasons, Bush's stance on Iraq, absent a congressional declaration, raises serious questions about his willingness to submit to the law of the land.

Finally, I cite the president's remarks in a speech given on February 26, 2003, to the American Enterprise Institute.[28] Had I not known who made these remarks I might have thought a petty tyrant was speaking, not the leader of the Free World. Read them and decide for yourself whether these are the words of an empire-builder or a public servant:

"We meet here during a crucial period in the history of our nation, and of the civilized world. Part of that history was written by others; the rest will be written by us."

"The rest [of history] will be written by us"? That's an absurdity!

"And we set a goal: we will not allow the triumph of hatred and violence in the affairs of men."

Bush clearly believes that government can solve the greatest ills of mankind, and that political coercion will triumph.

"In Iraq, a dictator is building and hiding weapons that could enable him to dominate the Middle East and intimidate the civilized world—and we will not allow it. This same tyrant has close ties to terrorist organizations, and could supply them with the terrible means to strike this country—and America will not permit it. The danger posed by Saddam Hussein and his weapons cannot be ignored or wished away. The danger must be confronted."

An even greater threat to international stability is posed by North Korea led by a dictator and tyrant, but Bush knows when he's met his match.

"The United States has no intention of determining the precise form of Iraq's new government. That choice belongs to the Iraqi people. Yet, we will ensure that one brutal dictator is not replaced by another. All Iraqis must have a voice in the new government, and all citizens must have their rights protected."

Translation: America knows what's best for the Iraqi people. They'll get a democracy—even if they have to eat bullets in the process.

"The world has a clear interest in the spread of democratic values, because stable and free nations do not breed the ideologies of murder. They encourage the peaceful pursuit of a better life."

Has Bush forgotten what the U.S. government did to sister states that had peacefully seceded and sought a "better life" out of the

Union? It burned their cities and left their civilian populations to die from hunger and cold.

"The United States and other nations are working on a road map for peace."

Apparently Bush has forgotten his eschatology: only the Prince of Peace can bring freedom from strife to the world.

"We are a permanent member of the United Nations Security Council. We helped to create the Security Council. We believe in the Security Council—so much that we want its words to have meaning."

Bush forgot to mention his adamant refusal to allow the Security Council to fulfill its mandated role in terms of legitimizing military operations in Iraq.

"Yet, the security of our nation and the hope of millions depend on us, and Americans do not turn away from duties because they are hard. We have met great tests in other times, and we will meet the tests of our time."

The lack of secure borders and a failed immigration policy were largely responsible for the terrorist acts of 9/11, and our borders remain as porous as ever.

"We go forward with confidence, because we trust in the power of human freedom to change lives and nations. By the resolve and purpose of America, and of our friends and allies, we will make this an age of progress and liberty. Free people will set the course of history, and free people will keep the peace of the world."

Bush says "we trust in the power of human freedom to change lives and nations"? What about "In God We Trust"? He speaks of "an age of progress and liberty." This is secular humanism, pure and simple!

All of this is unbelievable hubris. Bush tried to convince the American public that the Iraqi people are not the enemy, only Saddam Hussein. But how do Iraqi citizens feel now that they have been confronted by an American military government running their own country? Like a conquered, subjugated people.

The resolution by Congress to give the president a semblance of legitimacy in pursuing a unilateral aggressive war will surely be remembered as one of the worst abdications of Congressional responsibility in our history, comparable to such colossal failures of government as the Gulf of Tonkin Resolution. Years from now, with Americans pinned down in a pan-Arab war, the chicken-hawks in Congress who allowed themselves to be duped will feel like fools. Alas, such is the price of hubris.

In 1999 candidate Bush said, "Let us not dominate others with our power. ... Let us have an American foreign policy that reflects American character. The modesty of true strength. The humility of real greatness. This is the strong heart of America. And this will be the spirit of my administration." Later in the presidential debates he expanded on the theme: "The United States must be humble. ... We must be proud and confident of our values, but humble in how we treat nations that are figuring out how to chart their own course." My question is this: What has happened to all that humility, that statesmanlike restraint, in Bush's addresses?

The Americanization of the Globe?

Believing with Jefferson that the government which governs best governs least, on the issue of the Iraqi war I side squarely with my libertarian friends, who have been among the staunchest allies of the old right in forging a foreign policy that keeps America out of wars where the vital interests of the republic are not threatened. When it comes to foreign affairs I believe the best thing America can do is to follow the sage advice of our first president, George Washington: "The great rule of conduct for us, in regard to foreign nations, is in extending our commercial relations to have with them as little political connections as possible."

Today we are seeing the very opposite taking place in our foreign policy. Indeed, if American interventionism continues at the current pace, there is absolutely no doubt in my mind that the conflict will rapidly degenerate into a two-continent war from Algeria to Iraq, with the United States and Israel left to fight alone against a half-dozen Arab and Muslim states. It's almost as if the Constitution doesn't exist anymore, not to mention the voice of our European allies, many of whom are vociferously calling for restraint, to no apparent avail.

In 1812, Great Britain didn't want war with America. We gave them one anyway. In 1861, the Confederate States of America were desperate to avoid a conflict if a way could be found to do so with honor. Lincoln had other plans. After the sinking of the *Lusitania*, Kaiser Wilhelm curtailed submarine warfare for two years to avoid bringing America into World War I. We came in anyway. As for World War II, why did Japan, with one tenth of our industrial power, launch a sneak attack on the U.S. fleet at Pearl Harbor and draw America into a war to the death? Were the Japanese insane? Hardly. The Japanese attacked Pearl Harbor only when our oil embargo left them no other way to avert an economic disaster at home. Finally, after our Cold War triumph, when we had a chance to beef up our defenses and reduce our international commitments, we did the opposite, expanding our obligations to Eastern Europe, the Balkans, the Gulf, and Central Asia, all the while reducing our armed forces by 50 percent.

Let's not forget that it's unconstitutional to go to war, even a "preemptive war," without a congressional declaration. On this issue, as on so many others, Pat Buchanan[29] is right: "Keep America the greatest power on earth, first on land, sea, in the air and space. Strike hard any enemy that strikes us. Hold high the torch of liberty, republicanism. But keep the bravest of America's young out of wars where no vital interest is at risk, and do not send our wealth abroad in foreign aid to balance the budgets of foreign regimes when we cannot even balance our own."

Meanwhile, I pray for a regime change—not one in Iraq necessarily, but one right here at home. I pray that Americans will have enough courage and sense to elect a president and Congress who will fulfill their solemn oaths of office and adhere strictly to the principles spelled out in the United States Constitution. And I pray for a return to George Washington's vision of friendly commerce with all and entangling alliances with none.

Our first parents desired the one thing forbidden them— autonomy. Thus hubris entered the human race, and the plague of pride has been with us ever since. Today I grieve over our national arrogance and wonder if God will ever grant us the willingness to repent. I ask you: Isn't that the root sin of our empire-crazed civilization? At L.A.'s *Shadow Convention* in July 2000, Senator John McCain said:[30] "I believe in American exceptionalism. I believe we were meant to transform history. I believe that the progress of all humanity will depend, as it has for many years now, on the global progress of American interests and values. I believe we are still the last, best hope of earth." What vanity! Yes, it is vanity to court honor with worldly potentates and to be puffed up with visions of grandeur. It is vanity to trust in the "progress of humanity" and in riches that perish. It is vanity to wish for long life and to care little about a well-lived life. Vanity of vanities, all is vanity, except to love God and serve Him in brokenness and humility!

Proverbs 16:18 says, "Pride goes before destruction, a haughty spirit before a fall." Writing to the church at Rome, Paul said, "Do not think of yourself more highly than you ought, but rather think of yourself with sober judgment" (Romans 12:3). Arrogant pride is despicable in the eyes of God. Only through God's help can we be the humble nation the Bible honors. As David prayed, "Search me, O God, and know my heart; test me and know my anxious thoughts. See if there is any offensive way in me, and lead me in the way everlasting" (Psalm 139:23, 24).

A wrongful pride has wormed its way into American society on a national level. Even when our pride is not openly blatant, because we intentionally hide its presence, it still saps the spiritual life that complete dependence on God provides. In an age of heady globalization, Americans no longer fear the Almighty. Tragically, it appears that we prefer instead the axis of hubris, the officious strut, the Brave New World.

— Chapter 8 —

The Issue of the Century:
Roy Moore and the Ten Commandments

Will the United States of America remain a constitutional republic? Or is she destined to succumb to the rule of a tyrannical judiciary? This is the issue of the century.

The options have been handed to us on a golden platter in the Alabama Ten Commandments case. On the one hand, some evangelical leaders have been outspoken in their support of former Alabama Chief Justice Roy Moore and strongly disagree with those who have criticized Moore's legal strategy. Others, however, insist that Moore should have obeyed a federal court order and removed the monument. They argue that court orders must be followed.

All this talk about obeying court orders is facile in the extreme. It reflects not only an appalling ignorance of our federal Constitution but a fatal misunderstanding of Moore's position. The Roy Moore case is most certainly about respecting the rule of law, but not about obeying an unconstitutional ruling. We must keep several considerations in mind.

1. The debate, at its core, is not about the Ten Commandments at all. It is about whether the people of the state of Alabama should be allowed to decide for themselves how they will express their religious convictions under the U.S. Constitution. Just as importantly, but on a much broader scale, the debate is over whether Americans are willing to pay the price to restore the federal government to its limited, delegated, constitutional functions, and American jurisprudence to its biblical foundations.

2. Despite what detractors of Judge Moore are saying about the importance of "obeying a judge's ruling" and "upholding the law," the root of the problem is a federal judiciary that is wildly out of control. Contrary to the plain text of the Constitution, the federal judiciary has erred in its conclusion that the First Amendment precludes the establishment of religion. In reality, the First Amendment is a guarantee that the people of the states would be *free from any sort of federal dictation whatsoever* on the issue of how religion is to be expressed by their state governments. The First Amendment states, "Congress shall make no law respecting an establishment of religion." Coupled with the Tenth Amendment, which says that any power not explicitly given to the federal government or prohibited to the states is reserved to the states and to the people, the First Amendment *bans* federal involvement with the issue of religious establishment.

3. It is hypocritical in the extreme for the U.S. Supreme Court, as the guardian of the federal Constitution, to refuse to support Moore's right to acknowledge God. When the U.S. Supreme Court is in session it opens its proceedings with the statement, "God save the United States and this honorable court." Both the U.S. Senate and House open their proceedings with a prayer given by a minister who is remunerated from the public treasury. Our national currency references God: "In God We Trust." Our founding documents do the same.

4. As noted above, the argument that Moore was "breaking the law" by refusing to obey a federal court injunction is hopelessly flawed no matter how many times it is asserted or by whom. No law

has been disobeyed, only a court ruling, and courts cannot make law, nor can they dictate through the arbitrary will of judges. Court rulings must be based either in (a) written law or (b) the U.S. Constitution. Court rulings without any basis in law or the Constitution are thus lawless rulings and must, in fact, be *dis*obeyed. Roy Moore was therefore both morally right and legally bound to refuse an unlawful court order that destroys the right of the people of Alabama, under the First and Tenth Amendments, to determine how religion will be expressed in their state.

5. The crisis in Alabama, as much as it is to be decried, is a golden opportunity for the nation. After decades of gross judicial abuse the constitutional crisis in America has finally come to a head. As we have seen, the U.S. Constitution bans any federal action whatsoever with respect to the issue of religious establishment, and all powers not given to the federal government are reserved to the states or to the people through their state governments. Because the federal courts have no jurisdiction in this matter, state officials are obligated to defend the rights of their people in their states. The only question is, will they rise to the occasion and do so? The people must see that they do.

6. The church cannot remain silent in the controversy. If it does, it will lose whatever credibility it still has in society. Pastors can and must use their pulpits to speak the truth about the abuses in the federal judiciary. At the same time, churches must come to grips with the fact that their 501(c)3 tax exempt status is nothing less than an attempt by the IRS to inhibit free speech and is fundamentally incompatible with the principles of religious freedom upon which our nation was established. It is a disgrace that so many pastors, for fear of losing their government-issued license to preach, are remaining silent in this hour of crisis. Government has no claim of authority whatsoever over God's church. It is the right and duty of pastors to demand that our government officials fulfill their pledge to defend the Constitution of the United States and to protect our Christian heritage.

7. The counter-revolution currently being waged by defenders of constitutional government is just getting underway and deserves the full support of all freedom-loving Americans. We must not let a courageous man who dared to defy tyranny stand alone against the hordes of political-correctness. We must join Roy Moore in saying, "Enough is enough! The line is drawn, and we are on the Lord's side!"

8. It is also time for Congress to stand up and be counted. Alexander Hamilton wrote in the Federalist Papers that he expected Congress to use its discretion to make exceptions and regulations to keep the judiciary "the least dangerous" of the three branches of government. If ever there was a time when Congress needed to protect the public from the usurpations of activist judges who are assaulting basic American principles it is now. Tragically, Congress has failed to fulfill its constitutional duty to keep the federal courts in their proper place.

In the final analysis, the crisis in Alabama is an opportunity for every one of us as individuals to declare where we stand, not only on this issue, but on the nature and purpose of civil government. I would like to state publicly and unequivocally my support for Roy Moore in his decision to uphold the law, and I urge all Christians to join me in praying that God would smile upon him and the people of Alabama as they seek to honor and obey the Divine Judge of the Universe.

"That Fox"

Meanwhile I have been fascinated by the chameleon-like metamorphosis undergone by Alabama Attorney General Bill Pryor. Supposedly a supporter of conservative causes, he decided that he must "uphold the law" and that Roy's Rock had to be removed from the state judiciary building in Montgomery. This reminds me of an episode that is recorded for us in the New Testament Gospels. The

Pharisees had warned Jesus that if He remained in Herod's territory His life would be in danger. They were, of course, trying to "help" Jesus keep out of trouble with the authorities. Naturally their well-intended "warning" failed to terrify Jesus. Instead He bids them tell Herod—"that fox"—that He intends to defy His threats (Luke 11:32). He will stay the course until His ministry is completed.

The word "fox" that Jesus used is an interesting term. Today it connotes cunning cleverness. Not so in Jesus' day. In its Jewish usage it had a double meaning. First, it referred to *low sneakiness* rather than straightforward dealing; and second, it was used in contrast to "lion" to describe an *unimportant and irrelevant person* as opposed to a person of real honor and greatness. In essence, Jesus was saying: "Folks, I am going to do what *the Father* has told Me to do. I will therefore make My way toward Jerusalem on *My* timing. I won't flee there. After all, I'm not a coward, and I'm certainly not dumb enough to fall for your machinations!"

It's apparent to many Moore supporters that Bill Pryor will do anything to help his nomination for a seat on the eleventh U.S. Circuit Court of Appeals. At least that's the opinion of the protestors who marched on Pryor's office to demand he resign for backing the eight associate justices who supported the removal of the Ten Commandments monument. As protest organizer Patrick Mahoney said, "Bill Pryor should be protecting the citizens of Alabama instead of campaigning to get confirmation on the eleventh Circuit." Pryor, like King Herod of old, certainly seems to be behaving like a "fox"—a sneaky and weak leader. He has joined Alabama Governor Bob Riley and members of the Supreme Court in deserting Moore in his hour of crisis. Little wonder that Moore has had to come out and publicly oppose him.

Commenting on the term "fox," G. Campbell Morgan once said: "It is an appalling picture. Jesus evaded Herod, sent him a message of contempt, and when face to face with him (at His trial before Herod) had nothing to say to Him. It is a solemnizing story. A man may get into such a condition when he yields to the base, that even Christ has nothing to say to him." Add to this the statement of Karl

Barth and you get a pretty good picture of where the battle lines are drawn in Alabama today: "Jesus would, in actual fact, have been an enemy of the state if He had *not* dared to call King Herod a 'fox' (Luke 13:32). If the State has perverted its God-given authority, it cannot be honored better than by this criticism which is due it in all circumstances."

Who would have thought the anti-God crowd would be joined by conservative Republicans! What could have motivated them to desert the U.S. Constitution? If the Republican leaders in Alabama think they can get away with this, they better think again. The conservative Christian vote is strong in 'Bama, and already plans are underway to defeat Pryor and Riley at the polls. Meanwhile, Riley's $1.2 billion tax plan was defeated in a statewide referendum in 2003, largely because Moore's supporters cast a protest vote.

Ah, the price of being a fox.

Defending Our Constitutional Rights

Once again, the issue is the United States Constitution. In an Op/Ed piece,[31] Roy Moore hit the nail on the head when he wrote: "By telling the state of Alabama that it may not acknowledge God, Judge Thompson effectively dismantled the justice system of the state. Judge Thompson never declared the Alabama Constitution unconstitutional, but the essence of his ruling was to prohibit judicial officers from obeying the very constitution they are sworn to uphold. In so doing, Judge Thompson and all who supported his order violated the rule of law."

The argument of Moore's opponents is thus turned on its head. Moore is hardly a lawbreaker, except to the extent that he is attempting to honor and obey a more fundamental law, the U.S. Constitution. Moore said:

Alabama Attorney General Bill Pryor and my fellow justices have argued that they must act to remove the monument to preserve the rule of law. But the precise opposite is true: Article VI of the Constitution makes explicitly clear that the Constitution, and the laws made pursuant to it, are "the supreme Law of the Land." Judge Thompson and the judges of the 11th U.S. Circuit Court of Appeals have all sworn oaths which bind them to support the Constitution as it is written— not as they would personally prefer it to be written. By subjugating the people of Alabama to the unconstitutional edict by Judge Thompson, that public officials may not acknowledge God, the attorney general and my colleagues have made the fiat opinion of a judge supreme over the text of the Constitution. While agreeing with me that the Constitution is supreme, and that the opinion of Judge Thompson was contrary to the Constitution, the attorney general has argued that he must follow an order he himself believes to be in direct violation of the supreme law of the land.

It might be helpful if Moore's critics would actually listen to what he has said. In deciding to disregard an *unlawful* order of a *federal* judge in a matter pertaining to the *state* of Alabama, Moore is guilty of "civil disobedience" only if we define the term according to Pharisaic sophistry. There is a higher law at stake. As Moore stated, his actions are "the lawful response of the highest judicial officer of the state to his oath of office," adding, "Had the judge declared the 13th Amendment prohibition on involuntary slavery to be illegal, or ordered the churches of my state burned to the ground, there would be little question in the minds of the people of Alabama and the U.S. that such actions should be ignored as unconstitutional and beyond the legitimate scope of a judge's authority. Judge Thompson's decision to unilaterally void the duties of elected officials under the state constitution and to prohibit judges from acknowledging God is equally unlawful."

In the end, it is Judge Thompson and his defenders who have put themselves above the law. The Moore case is but another tragic example of how our U.S. Constitution has become a worthless scrap of paper to many of our public officials.

Alabama's state motto declares, "Dare Defend Our Rights." I thank God that Roy Moore has been willing to do just that.

— Chapter 9 —

Cleanliness is Next to Impossible: Why Christians Must Get Down and Dirty in the Culture Wars

Believers in Jesus Christ are those who apply the lordship of Christ to every area of life—politics and prayer, government and church, society and spirituality. Institutions of human government comprise an integral part of the world into which Jesus sent His followers (John 17:18). They are to minister in this world as salt (Matt 5:13), light (Matt 5:14), and leaven (Matt 13:33). All of these metaphors point to transformation by penetration, change by involvement—not isolation. Just as salt interacts with meat to flavor or preserve it, light infiltrates darkness to dispel it, and leaven mixes with the lump to expand it, so Christians are to penetrate the world, government included, with the gospel.

While the Christian experience is always personal, it is never private. Confessing "Jesus is Lord" inevitably intermingles with counterclaims made by earthly potentates and the allegiance demanded by civil authorities. As citizens of two realms—the earthly and the spiritual—Christians must understand that their dual citizenship includes rights and responsibilities in both. This is what the apostle Paul was saying when he wrote to the Philippians: "The only thing that matters is...that you behave as good citizens [of heaven] in a manner worthy of the gospel" (Phil 1:27). The verb translated "behave as good citizens," *politeuomai*, means more than "conduct yourselves" or "live" (so most translations). Paul is reminding the Philippians that they are a new community in Christ in the midst of a Roman military colony. They are citizens of a new order of being that will continue while Rome's will crumble entirely. They are to live in the midst of the old order as worthy citizens of the new one.

It is this concept of dual citizenship that is the biblical basis for civic participation by Christians. In the New Testament the believer's civic obligation is emphatically commended alongside the obligation to serve God. "Render to Caesar the things that are Caesar's, and to God the things that are God's," said Jesus (Mark 12:17)—a thought echoed by the apostle Peter when in one breath he says, "Fear God; honor the emperor" (1 Pet 2:17). Hence, while Scripture pictures believers as pilgrims on earth passing through a foreign country on their way home, it forbids them to be indifferent to matters of human government. As J. I. Packer has said: "The more profoundly one is concerned about heaven, the more deeply one cares about God's will being done on earth."

Of course, there are dangers to be avoided, most notably the politicized intentions of the social gospel movement as represented by the more liberal Protestant denominations, and the pietistic "come-out-ism" of some Christian separatists. Neither will do. The goals of Christianity can never be reduced to a socio-political scheme whereby God's kingdom will be established on earth through political activism alone. The Bible declares Jesus Christ to be, first and foremost, our Savior from sin, delivering us from the wrath to come. His kingdom is not of this world in the sense that what we experience in this life as Christians is preparatory for the life to come. However, neither will pietistic separatism do, which often takes the form of political passivity and unwillingness to be involved in any level of civic activity. The root problem with this view is a faulty eschatology that sees the world as getting inevitably worse until the coming of Christ and tells us, therefore, that there is nothing we can do about it. Whatever truth there is in this view (and there is much truth in it), and however true it is that evangelism should always be our first concern, there remains a social and political task for the Christian, as Jesus, Paul, and Peter said.

The most serious threats to the American way of life do not come from overt opposition or hostility—not yet, at least. The most serious problems are the realities of an ever-expanding federal government that squeezes freedom out on a piecemeal basis—regulation by regulation—justified by "public policy concerns" or "compelling state interests." As many paleoconservatives and libertarians point out, the regulatory state can be just as destructive as the hostile state. In fact, the regulatory state can often be worse because at least the hostile state is open about its opposition and invites prophetic response and, when necessary, civil disobedience ("We must obey God rather than man").

If there is one thing history has taught us, it is that the state that is out to do "good" is the most dangerous of all. Congressman Ron Paul[32] (R-TX) has noted: "Most of the damage to liberty and the Constitution is done by men and women of good will who are convinced they know what is best for the economy, for others, and foreign powers. They inevitably fail to recognize their own arrogance in assuming they know what is the best personal behavior for others. Their failure to recognize the likelihood of mistakes by central planners allows them to ignore the magnitude of a flawed central government directive, compared to an individual or a smaller unit of government mistake." Likewise, C. S. Lewis observes the dangers of "do-goodism": "Of all tyrannies a tyranny sincerely exercised for the good of its victim may be the most oppressive. It may be better to live under robber barons than under omnipotent moral busybodies. The robber baron's cruelty may sometimes sleep, his cupidity may at some point be satiated, but those who torment us for our own good will torment us without end for they do so with the approval of their own conscience."

There is no doubt that from a biblical viewpoint the republican form of government as originally established in America is a fitter and wiser form than any other the world has even known. By limiting the power of elected officials, it correctly acknowledges the fallenness of human nature and the tendency, as Lord Acton put it, for power to corrupt and for absolute power to corrupt absolutely. Evangelical Christianity as a whole has always repudiated state absolutism, which imposes on the masses the whim of political tyrants. Thus, when Christians speak out against a bloated federal bureaucracy, what they are undermining is not civil government per se, but false gods and a counterfeit vision of freedom and justice.

Dietrich Bonhoeffer and the Cost of Discipleship

Nazi Germany provides us with a classic example of state power run amok. I have always been fascinated—and put to shame—by the courageous example of the young German theologian Dietrich Bonhoeffer (1906-1945). Our life paths have been similar in some respects. He belonged to a music-loving family and enjoyed athletics. He had a talent for learning foreign languages and took an early interest in theology. He was blessed with a good university education (his was Tübingen, mine Basel). He traveled widely. In fact, it was during a visit to Libya that he was confronted for the first time with the brutal logic and incomprehensibility of war. The decision to pursue a theological career was not an easy one for him, but it was always his relationship with God that gave him the most joy and satisfaction in life.

There the similarities end. Dietrich Bonhoeffer is justly remembered not only as one of the greatest theologians of the twentieth century but also as a courageous individual of faith. For participating in the conspiracy to kill Adolf Hitler, Bonhoeffer was executed by the Nazis at Flössenburg Concentration Camp in the last month of World War II. He had been arrested two years earlier for helping 14 Jews escape to Switzerland. What led him to risk it all?

Few would have thought that the Nationalsozialistische Deutsche Arbeiter-Partie, starting as a gang of unemployed soldiers in 1919, would become the legal government of Germany by 1933. In fourteen short years, Adolf Hitler, a once obscure corporal, emerged to become the Chancellor of Germany. World War I had ended in 1918 with a total of 37 million casualties, including nine million dead combatants. German propaganda had ill prepared the nation for defeat, resulting in a sense of injured national pride. The military and political leaders who were responsible for the defeat claimed that Germany had been "stabbed in the back" by its leftwing politicians, Communists, and Jews. When the Weimar Republic tried to establish a democratic course, political parties from both the right and the left struggled for control, at times violently. The new regime could handle neither the depressed economy nor the rampant lawlessness. Into this void appeared Hitler and the Nazi Party, promising to right all wrongs and reestablish Germany as a great national power.

In his discussion of the church in Nazi Germany,[33] Professor Michael Moeller shows how Bonhoeffer's religious contemporaries succumbed to the delusion that the church had to be ushered into Nazism. As Moeller puts it, "To speak against what was regarded as a proper Germanization of the church evoked passionate opposition in a time when the majority of the populace was drunk with nationalism." For Bonhoeffer, however, the gospel could never be found in worldly ideologies.

On May 28, 1933, Bonhoeffer preached a sermon in the Kaiser Wilhelm Memorial Church in Berlin. It was a defining moment in history. The Nazis had just seized power and were tightening their grip on the nation. Political developments happened quickly in the first five months of Nazi rule in Germany. As Moeller has shown, the Nazi takeover was a textbook example of a revolutionary movement's successful exploitation of an unstable situation to consolidate its power. Moeller summarizes the chronology of events as follows:

> **January 30, 1933:** Hitler sworn in as Chancellor of Germany.
> **February 27, 1933:** The Reichstag set on fire.
> **February 28, 1933:** A State of Emergency proclaimed.
> **March 23, 1933:** "Law for Removing the Distress of People and Reich" ("Enabling Act") enacted. Legislative power transferred to the Executive.
> **April 7, 1933:** "Law to Harmonize the State Governments and National Authority" enacted and the federal structure dissolved.

The "Enabling Act" curtailed the constitutional freedoms of Germans, based on peril to the homeland, with a promise that they would be fully restored in four years. The German parliament, which was similar to our U.S. House and Senate, was also promised that the new powers used would be only those "essential for carrying out vitally necessary measures" for the protection of the state and people, and that the "recourse to such a law [would be] in itself a limited one."

In bringing about these sweeping changes, the Nazi government enjoyed broad support from the public. After the chaotic end of the twenties and Germany's terrible economic crisis, it seemed that national pride was finally possible again. Law and order had been restored. Hitler was regarded by many as the new Führer (leader) who would bring Germany out of the chaos of the Weimar republic and create a stable society.

As Moeller notes, Hitler's rapid ascendancy was greeted with enthusiasm by church leaders who felt that the radical change in the nation's political system should also take place in the church. If the new Germany needed a new leader, the church also needed a new Reichsbishof (national bishop) to usher it into the new era. The party working for the Nazification of the church called itself the Deutsche Christen (German Christians). In this movement, Hitler was considered a German "prophet," and racial consciousness was considered a source of revelation alongside the Bible. The German Christians affirmed Hitler as a new Messiah and accepted Nazism's anti-Semitism. It was in reaction to the excesses of the German Christians that another group, calling itself the Confessing Church, was formed, chiefly out of the Lutheran and Reformed churches. The Confessing Church took its name because it clung to the church's great historical confessions of faith. The Barmen Declaration was the work of this group, written at its initial synod in Barmen, Germany, in May 1934. Although the declaration focused on concern for the church and ecclesiastical renewal, it was also considered a political document with clear political implications. This is obvious even in the initial affirmation, which reads, "Jesus Christ, as he is attested for us in Holy Scripture, is the one Word of God whom we have to hear and whom we have to trust and obey in life and in death." This affirmation is meant to motivate Christians to greater trust and obedience, regardless of the consequences—and the signers of the declaration knew that the costs might be high.

Bonhoeffer, now an ordained pastor, immediately distanced himself from the German Christians and their program. In his sermon of May 28, 1933, Bonhoeffer addresses the changes being advocated by the German Christians. Basing his sermon on the story of the Golden Calf in Exodus 32, Bonhoeffer distinguishes between the church of Aaron and the church of Moses. The church of Aaron, he says, is the church of this world. It answers the demands of humans by encouraging them to go their own selfish ways. The Aaron church may well ask for sacrifices, but the sacrifices themselves are self-serving. The Aaron church is the church of idols and will ultimately be destroyed by God, because "in the cross all making of gods, all idolatry comes to an end. The whole of humanity, the whole church is judged and pardoned. Here God is God." The statist fervor of the

German Christians impelled Bonhoeffer to say that the true church must constantly defend itself against idolatry. Long before the excesses of the Third Reich forced Bonhoeffer to join the political resistance, acceptance by the German Christians of Nazi ideology had driven him into a state of protest against the church in which they were so dominant.

What, then, was the role of the pastor for Bonhoeffer? And what is the responsibility of church leaders today? Moeller, who carefully studied this issue, concluded: "The pastor has to speak the truth. Not the truth of ideologies, but the truth of the Gospel which the world does not like to hear. The role of the pastor is not to be the master of ceremonies for the world celebrating itself. The role of the pastor might be more the role of the fool, the one who is set aside to speak the truth even though nobody really wants to hear it."

Bonhoeffer's decision to join the plot against Hitler wasn't an easy one. But his realization that the truth requires suffering enabled him to take the fateful step. "I believe that God can and wants to create good out of everything, even evil," he said. "For that he needs people who use everything for the best. I believe that God provides us with as much strength to resist in every calamity as we need. But he does not give it in advance, so that we trust him alone. In such a trust all anxiety about the future must be overcome."

Do We Need a New Barmen Declaration?

George Orwell arrived at the title of his novel about totalitarianism by reversing the last two digits of the year in which it was published. Ever since then, *1984* has become a symbol describing a dreadful world of thought control. Interestingly, 1984 was also the 50th anniversary of the Confessing Church's Barmen Declaration that was issued in 1934, well into Hitler's second year in power. This declaration was one of only a handful of challenges to what the Nazis were doing in Germany.

The German people had sinfully acknowledged that truth was to be found only in the Nazi Party—apart from "the one Word of God." Germany's salvation was now located in Nazi ideology. Racial purity and anti-Semitism were now the twin "truths" of German society. For the signers of the Barmen Declaration, to accept Jesus Christ meant to reject these "truths" and especially Adolf Hitler. The same attitude was taken by Martin Niemöller in a book he published during this period entitled "Christus ist mein Führer," or *Christ Is My Leader*. The use of the term "Führer" was intentional, since everybody in Germany referred to Hitler by that title. For Niemöller, "Christ is my Führer" implied its negation, "Hitler is *not* my Führer," and for stating this Niemöller spent seven years in Dachau. The signatories of the Barmen Declaration clearly felt that they were living in a time when the true church could no longer say, "We affirm both Christ and Hitler." They had to proclaim, in effect, "The debate about Hitler is now closed. We have rendered our verdict. The matter is no longer negotiable."

Are we in America actually facing, or are we close to facing, a similar situation? The indications that we may be on our way to a totalitarian society concern mainly our doctrine of national security. With the United States engaged in the military occupation of Iraq, our president emphatically insists that the necessity of a war against that sovereign nation was based on a real and imminent threat against the United States of America, despite compelling evidence to the contrary. We are told that in the interest of national security we must all be willing to sacrifice our personal freedoms in the name of the Patriot Act and other measures that reduce the Bill of Rights to a worthless scrap of paper. In the name of security we are told that a government must not let its people know too much or they will be in danger of losing their influence in the world.

A spirit of wild jingoism seems to have infected the Bush administration. Men who are supposed to look at world events in a calm and dispassionate way now talk only of "war" and "liberation," as though these were the sole thoughts of the American people. If you attempt to argue with such gentlemen they will tell you that you don't know what you're talking about, accuse you of unpatriotic conduct, and sneer at your reasonings and conclusions. I cannot help but feel that a rude awakening is in store for these self-constituted apostles of freedom and humanity.

One of the most disturbing recent examples of this attitude has been the Bush administration's willingness to used flawed intelligence to make its case for the invasion of Iraq. Bush's posture on the war—including the fact that he invaded Iraq without constitutional authority to do so—is the beginning of what appears to be a growing totalitarian mentality that says, "We are above the law. We are not accountable to a world body or even to our own government. We don't need to tell people what we are doing, and we will accuse those who challenge us, even in Congress, of making us weak."

The Barmen Declaration claimed that there is only "one Word of God whom we have to hear, and whom we have to trust and obey in life and in death." For Christians, that Word is Jesus Christ. In the name of that same God it may become necessary for us to protest today, as the signers of the Barmen Declaration did in 1934, when the leaders of our government say, "Hear, trust and obey us in life and in death. We'll tell you what to think. If we withhold information, it's for your own good. And if our arguments don't make sense, be assured that there are reasons behind them that we can't share with you." When government says such things, it begins to look frighteningly like a Caesar trying to elicit unquestioning and docile loyalty from an unthinking populace. Government becomes a god, and demands to be worshipped as such. As that begins to happen, our response must be to say no because we have already said yes to the one Word of God whom we are obligated to trust and obey in life and in death. For both Bonhoeffer and Niemöller, action by the church was justified on the basis of ensuring that the state fulfilled its God-given function as state and not as god. Tragically, the Confessing Church in Germany acted too late. I hope we do not repeat their tardiness.

Beware of the New Patriotism

America is but a fleeting actor on the stage of history. As Walter Lippmann once put it: "When Shakespeare was alive, there were no Americans; when Virgil was alive, there were no Englishmen; when Homer was alive, there were no Romans." Much of what I have said in this book is addressed to my fellow conservatives, trying to review the biblical truths that gave birth to this nation and the political blunders that have led us off the pathway. Here I want to direct my comments particularly to pastors and other Christians in every state across the land.

Our forefathers founded this nation on principles basic to our Judeo-Christian heritage. And their greatest fear for the future of the nation was that one day the people would turn from these principles. That day has come. Christ demands our complete devotion, but the church has lapsed into a Christianity of custom and tradition. The result is that the church has allowed itself to be used for worldly purposes. Well-meaning but deceived believers are working around the clock to assimilate church and state. I would rather the church be thinned down to a tiny band and go into the catacombs than make a compact with this doctrine! Whoever today preaches a Christianity rooted in American nationality binds God's Word to an arbitrarily conceived *Weltanschauung*, thereby invalidating it, and places himself outside the evangelical church. Whoever talks this way imagines that he is able to serve both Yahweh and Mammon, which is utterly impossible.

The evangelical church of today deserves sharp criticism for its flabby, compromising attitude toward what I call the New Patriotism and because of its enthusiasm for the nation's arrogant empire-building. Under the guise of contending for liberty it is actually perpetuating the old compromise of nationalism and gospel. Paganism in the form of state worship has invaded the church, yet its leaders are silent. We who proclaim the Good News owe it to our congregations to oppose this falsification of the gospel with all of our being.

123

In this light, I have four brief suggestions to offer. First, the New Patriotism/Neo-Paganism is to be protested against because it is heresy and because it has become the prevailing doctrine in the church through usurpation. Secondly, the protest has to be directed fundamentally against the source of all errors, namely, that adherents to the New Patriotism place their faith in government as a second source of redemption, and thereby show themselves to be believers in another God. Thirdly, the protest can be raised only where there is a clear agreement about the essence of this sickness. And finally, all this should take place within the bosom of the church and in such a way as to call the church and its individual members to repentance.

The choice to become actively involved in politics is costly. Speak out on public issues, and the road you travel will become bumpy indeed. But who ever said the Christian life was easy? No one has put this better than Leslie Newbigin in his book, *The Other Side of 1984*:[34]

> Christian discipleship is a following of Jesus in the power of his risen life on the way which he went. That way is neither the way of purely interior spiritual pilgrimage, nor is it the way of realpolitik for the creation of a new social order. It goes the way that Jesus went, right into the heart of the world's business and politics, with a claim which is both uncompromising and vulnerable. It looks for a world of justice and peace, not as the product of its own action but as the gift of God who raises the dead and "calls into existence the things that do not exist" (Rom. 4:17). It looks for the holy city not as the product of its policies but as the gift of God. Yet it knows that to seek escape from politics into a private spirituality would be to turn one's back on the true city. It looks for the city "whose builder and maker is God," but it knows that the road to the city goes down out of sight, the way Jesus went, into that

dark valley where both our selves and all our works must disappear and be buried under the rubble of history. It therefore does not invest in any political programme...the hope and expectations of which belong properly only to the city which God has promised.

When you come to a fork in the road, take it, said Yogi Berra. America is indeed at a fork in the road. Our nation's history is filled with devout men and women who made an impact on government. Today it is up to Christians like you and me to get on our knees and pray, educate ourselves, and mobilize for action. If we are to win the culture war, we must become salt, light, and leaven in the political arena.

— *Chapter 10* —

What Easter Teaches Us

America has entered the greatest crisis in her history. Something has gone desperately wrong. Something is broken. Something has to be fixed. Where can we turn for a spark of optimism and a ray of sunshine?

We cannot turn to science. Science can instruct us on how to walk on the moon, but it cannot tell us how to walk on earth. The major concern of modern science is how to stay alive rather than on how to live.

Nor can we turn to politics. Heads of state make inspirational speeches and produce solemn documents and confer at world summits, but their agreements are worthless scraps of paper and their peace proposals are useless museum pieces. Politics can never be the answer because it foolishly tries to carve a lasting brotherhood out of the rotten wood of unregenerate humanity.

Religion likewise holds no hope for us. America is full of baptized pagans. Not even Christianity is the answer if by Christianity we mean "Churchianity," a kind of politically correct American denomination—"Christianity Lite," if you will. The rich young ruler of Luke 18:22 was probably a good person with a fine record but he lacked one thing: eternal life. He needed to forsake his worldly moorings and burn his bridges behind him completely. In short, he needed to be completely sold out to Jesus ("sell *all* that thou hast," said Christ).

Many Americans are like that rich young ruler. They regularly attend church, sit politely in their pews, and go through the motions of singing hymns and choruses, but their fingers are crossed. They have no intention of selling out to the Lord who bought them. To them religion is a good thing, but they will not be known for their radicalism. "No Sir, by golly, a calm moderation is what we need today."

Such people make absolutely no impact in today's world. The reason, says Paul in Romans 12:1-2, is that they allow themselves to be conformed to the thought patterns of the present age. The world system has squeezed them into its mold. The question Paul wishes to ask is this: *To what standards do you conform? And are you willing to break with those patterns of life that are ungodly, immoral, unsound, or unbiblical?* In short, he says, are you willing to be sanctified, to be changed from the inside out? Sanctification is a revolutionary process. It affects the very center of our consciousness. It is not a second blessing but a constant renewal. It is nothing other than the restoration of the divine image (*imago dei*) that was marred but not lost at the fall of Adam.

Today we confuse sanctification—the transformation of our thoughts and behavior—with modern-day fads or practical mysticism. We plod along with an occasional prayer for guidance, but having the mind of Christ means practically nothing in our daily experience. Stagnation, complacency, status quo thinking—all these characterize our lives. Islam is sweeping the world because at its center is a core of men and women completely sold out to the cause. A genuine Christian is sold out, not merely to a cause, or to a church, or to a religion, but to a Person—to Christ Himself. The Scripture calls for repentance from worldliness but we are in no mood for that. Nothing will avail until the saints become as desperate as the situation and voluntarily seek the Lord. All other options are vain though they may speak the language of the church.

Jesus did not pay so great a price merely to inaugurate a polite religious society that can effortlessly compromise with a godless age. On the contrary, He declared, "Do you think that I have come to bring peace on earth? No, I tell you; but division" (Luke 12:51). What a far cry from the cheap brand of politically correct Christianity so prevalent today! And I wonder how much longer evangelicals will grovel in their attempts to accommodate the world? The church needs agitators, men who will cooperate with God in arousing His people. Paul and his missionary helpers greatly troubled Philippi. They created no little stir in Ephesus. The early believers were accused of turning the world upside down. Christians are not called to sing lullabies but to sound the trumpet.

Our Lord said, "He that is not with Me is against Me, and he that gathers not with Me scatters abroad" (Matthew 12:30). The greatest menace in America today is not extremism but moderation, that middle-of-the-road tolerance that boasts of its broad-mindedness. We work both sides of the street. We meekly accept peaceful co-existence. But it is worse to be on the fence than to be on the wrong side of the fence. The Lord would have us cold or hot but not lukewarm.

At the bottom of the bottom line, the crisis in America is a crisis of fidelity. And the answer to a crisis of fidelity is fidelity: a deeper trust in God, a more thorough conviction of our position in Christ ("stand fast, therefore, in the liberty wherewith Christ hath set us free"), and a return to the clear teachings of the Word of God.

Of one thing we can be certain. The answer to the present crisis will not be found in Christianity Lite. It will only be found in classic Christianity—a Christianity with the courage to be countercultural, a Christianity that has reclaimed the wisdom of the past in order to face the corruptions of the present and create a renewed future, a Christianity that risks the high adventure of fidelity.

Easter teaches us that the Christian life is not a vacation but a vocation. We are participants, not spectators. It is a scandal for a man to be entertained when he should be enlisted. When God moves, we must rise to meet Him. Remember that courage, like cowardice, is a habit of the heart. And when the choice comes down to the cross or capitulation, may we be willing to take up the cross and lead.

— Chapter 11 —

Conclusion: An Urgent Appeal to All Freedom-Loving Americans

As you may have heard, the U.S. is putting together a constitution for Iraq. Why don't we just give them ours? Think about it—it was written by very smart people, it's served us well for over two hundred years, and besides, we're not using it anymore.

— *Tonight Show* host Jay Leno

It has been said that America's most original contribution to political theory has been the fact that it has no theory. In one sense that is true. American political thought is an aggregation of slogans, phrases, shibboleths, and traditions that has never been reduced to a single doctrine, unless one wishes to follow the example of Procrustes.

Yet our Founders, whose leading ideas were incorporated into the charter that was to become the cornerstone of American political institutions, were not ignorant of political theory. Together they rejected the mystically based state. Because they felt that human nature could not be trusted where political power was concerned, they produced a Constitution with a system of strict checks and balances. The federal Constitution was based on the assumption that men were not angels. Government was therefore to be laic, libertarian, and limited. These ideas are seen not only in the Constitution but also in our most notable quasi-official documents such as the Declaration of Independence and Washington's Farewell Address.

Today, however, an entire generation of Americans has grown up without a clear picture of our republican history. Our schools fail to teach children the Declaration of Independence and the principles of the Constitution. Few Americans understand the foundation for our freedoms. Even less do they understand where our freedoms are threatened today. Freedom as a pervasive ideal and goal as incorporated in the great documents of American life has been replaced by government mendaciousness and coercion. The traditional emphasis upon freedom *from* government intervention has been replaced by the extreme of the warfare/welfare state. The American ideal, once rooted in the concept of personal freedom and limited government, has become a shabby and despised creature. The philosophy of "the less government we have the better" no longer permeates the American mind and attitude.

Nowhere is this confusion more obvious today than in American foreign policy. The coalition forces in Iraq defend their occupation on two main grounds: on the basis of America's "self-interest" in the Middle East and on the "threat" to American national security posed by Islamist terrorist groups. In pursuing these goals there is no problem if we send our sons to die for an undeclared and unconstitutional war, or if we waste billions of taxpayers' dollars on rebuilding a nation that has the second largest oil reserve in the world, or if Saddam didn't plan the attacks on America, or if the president misled the public when he said we were in "imminent" danger from WMD (which, after months of searching, are still missing). Surely the irony is not lost on the American public. Bush wants to write a constitution for Iraq while freely breaking our own.

In no other country in the world—not even in Blair's Britain—is there such contempt for the spirit of '76. For better or for worse, U.S. presidents can serve as teachers to the nation, both by precept and example. If nothing else, Bush has helped crystallize world opinion concerning the use of American power and the meaning of the balance of power in international relations. What his next step will be, no one can know. But one thing is certain: The consequences of the Bush foreign policy for the future of America will be incalculable.

In this book I have suggested that the conditions in current American society and their causes are not something an external enemy did to the American people. We did it to ourselves via submission to a totalitarian-leaning Leviathan. As a result, America hardly resembles a republic anymore. In fact, our media often refer to the United States as a democracy. Thomas Jefferson said that a democracy (Latin for mob rule) was the worst form of government on earth and that we should avoid a democratic form of government like the plague. A republic is what our Founders gave us, not a democracy.

If you had told me this a few years ago I probably would have said, "So what?" Since that time I have learned the difference between a democracy and a republic. An example would be if we had 100 people in our country and 51 of them decided to hang the other 49. In a democracy, the 49 would hang (mob rule), but in a republic there would be a law that no one was to be hung, and therefore no one would hang. That's the difference between a democracy and a republic.

It was when I realized this vital truth that my thinking about government began to change. I understood for the first time that the U.S. Constitution established, not a popular democracy, but the rule of law in America. It was designed by the Founders to set up a small national government to do very limited acts for us and to keep us free from the domination of would-be tyrants. Constitutional government in our American republic was designed to allow us to enjoy the freedoms our Creator bestowed upon us.

The Constitution is as timeless as the hills and as relevant as our daily newspaper; it will serve us well into the future if we let it. But this will never happen unless we breathe life back into it and give it a fair chance. There's an old adage that says: "When you do nothing, something always happens." If you never fed your dog, I don't think it would last very long—if it bothered to hang around. If you never put oil in your car, I don't think it would take very long before your car would quit running. If you never mowed your lawn, the grass would just keep on growing until your yard became a jungle.

By the same token, if we do not care for, nurture, and guard our Constitution (remember, it is *ours*), it will be stolen out from under us. It's time we relegated this thing called government to the place it deserves in our lives, and that place is most certainly not to be a dictator. It's time we held civil magistrates accountable to the revealed law of God. Above all, it's time we acknowledged that true liberty and justice are found only "under God."

Remember, you and I are responsible for letting government falsely assume sovereignty over us. We have abdicated the responsibility of running the political part of our lives and given it to someone else to do for us instead of doing it for ourselves. We have invited the foxes into the coop, and—guess what?—the foxes have done what foxes always do: they have eaten our chickens. What's so unusual about that?

If there's one thing July 4, 1776, proved, it's that tyranny never corrects itself. History also shows that once a government tries to hold its sinking ship together with force, that force itself only hastens the demise of that government. And things will only get worse until enough of us raise a large enough hue and cry to make our politicians realize they can't get away with it forever. Isn't it time to put a halt to all the misery and suffering the abuse and neglect of the Constitution has wrought in our great republic? Isn't it time for *you* to join the American patriot movement?

THE DECLARATION OF INDEPENDENCE

July 4, 1776

The Unanimous Declaration of the Thirteen United States of America.

When, in the course of human events, it becomes necessary for one people to dissolve the political bonds which have connected them with another, and to assume among the powers of the earth, the separate and equal station to which the laws of nature and of nature's God entitle them, a decent respect to the opinions of mankind requires that they should declare the causes which impel them to the separation.

We hold these truths to be self-evident, that all men are created equal, that they are endowed by their Creator with certain unalienable rights, that among these are life, liberty and the pursuit of happiness. That to secure these rights, governments are instituted among men, deriving their just powers from the consent of the governed. That whenever any form of government becomes destructive to these ends, it is the right of the people to alter or to abolish it, and to institute new government, laying its foundation on such principles and organizing its powers in such form, as to them shall seem most likely to effect their safety and happiness.

Prudence, indeed, will dictate that governments long established should not be changed for light and transient causes; and accordingly all experience hath shown that mankind are more disposed to suffer, while evils are sufferable, than to right themselves by abolishing the forms to which they are accustomed. But when a long train of abuses and usurpations, pursuing invariably the same object evinces a design to reduce them under absolute despotism, it is their right, it is their duty, to throw off such government, and to provide new guards for their future security. — Such has been the patient sufferance of these colonies; and such is now the necessity which constrains them to alter their former systems of government. The history of the present King of Great Britain is a history of repeated injuries and usurpations, all having in direct object the establishment of an absolute tyranny over these states.

To prove this, let facts be submitted to a candid world.

He has refused his assent to laws, the most wholesome and necessary for the public good.

He has forbidden his governors to pass laws of immediate and pressing importance, unless suspended in their operation till his assent should be obtained; and when so suspended, he has utterly neglected to attend to them.

He has refused to pass other laws for the accommodation of large districts of people, unless those people would relinquish the right of representation in the legislature, a right inestimable to them and formidable to tyrants only.

He has called together legislative bodies at places unusual, uncomfortable, and distant from the depository of their public records, for the sole purpose of fatiguing them into compliance with his measures.

He has dissolved representative houses repeatedly, for opposing with manly firmness his invasions on the rights of the people.

He has refused for a long time, after such dissolutions, to cause others to be elected; whereby the legislative powers, incapable of annihilation, have returned to the people at large for their exercise; the state remaining in the meantime exposed to all the dangers of invasion from without, and convulsions within.

He has endeavored to prevent the population of these states; for that purpose obstructing the laws for naturalization of foreigners;

refusing to pass others to encourage their migration hither, and raising the conditions of new appropriations of lands.

He has obstructed the administration of justice, by refusing his assent to laws for establishing judiciary powers.

He has made judges dependent on his will alone, for the tenure of their offices, and the amount and payment of their salaries.

He has erected a multitude of new offices, and sent hither swarms of officers to harass our people, and eat out their substance.

He has kept among us, in times of peace, standing armies without the consent of our legislature.

He has affected to render the military independent of and superior to civil power.

He has combined with others to subject us to a jurisdiction foreign to our constitution, and unacknowledged by our laws; giving his assent to their acts of pretended legislation:

For quartering large bodies of armed troops among us:

For protecting them, by mock trial, from punishment for any murders which they should commit on the inhabitants of these states:

For cutting off our trade with all parts of the world:

For imposing taxes on us without our consent:

For depriving us in many cases, of the benefits of trial by jury:

For transporting us beyond seas to be tried for pretended offenses:

For abolishing the free system of English laws in a neighboring province, establishing therein an arbitrary government, and enlarging its boundaries so as to render it at once an example and fit instrument for introducing the same absolute rule in these colonies:

For taking away our charters, abolishing our most valuable laws, and altering fundamentally the forms of our governments:

For suspending our own legislatures, and declaring themselves invested with power to legislate for us in all cases whatsoever.

He has abdicated government here, by declaring us out of his protection and waging war against us.

He has plundered our seas, ravaged our coasts, burned our towns, and destroyed the lives of our people.

He is at this time transporting large armies of foreign mercenaries to complete the works of death, desolation and tyranny, already begun with circumstances of cruelty and perfidy scarcely paralleled in the most barbarous ages, and totally unworthy the head of a civilized nation.

He has constrained our fellow citizens taken captive on the high seas to bear arms against their country, to become the executioners of their friends and brethren, or to fall themselves by their hands.

He has excited domestic insurrections amongst us, and has endeavored to bring on the inhabitants of our frontiers, the merciless Indian savages, whose known rule of warfare, is undistinguished destruction of all ages, sexes and conditions.

In every stage of these oppressions we have petitioned for redress in the most humble terms: our repeated petitions have been answered only by repeated injury. A prince, whose character is thus marked by every act which may define a tyrant, is unfit to be the ruler of a free people.

Nor have we been wanting in attention to our British brethren.

We have warned them from time to time of attempts by their legislature to extend an unwarrantable jurisdiction over us.

We have reminded them of the circumstances of our emigration and settlement here.

We have appealed to their native justice and magnanimity, and we have conjured them by the ties of our common kindred to disavow these usurpations, which, would inevitably interrupt our connections and correspondence.

We must, therefore, acquiesce in the necessity, which denounces our separation, and hold them, as we hold the rest of mankind, enemies in war, in peace friends.

We, therefore, the representatives of the United States of America, in General Congress, assembled, appealing to the Supreme Judge of the world for the rectitude of our intentions, do, in the name, and by the authority of the good people of these colonies, solemnly publish and declare, that these united colonies are, and of right ought to be free and independent states; that they are absolved from all allegiance to the British Crown, and that all political connection between them and the state of Great Britain, is and ought to be totally dissolved; and that as free and independent states, they have full power to levy war, conclude peace, contract alliances, establish commerce, and to do all other acts and things which independent states may of right do. And for the support of this declaration, with a firm reliance on the protection of Divine Providence, we mutually pledge to each other our lives, our fortunes and our sacred honor.

New Hampshire: Josiah Bartlett, William Whipple, Matthew Thornton
Massachusetts: John Hancock, Samual Adams, John Adams, Robert Treat Paine, Elbridge Gerry
Rhode Island: Stephen Hopkins, William Ellery
Connecticut: Roger Sherman, Samuel Huntington, William Williams, Oliver Wolcott
New York: William Floyd, Philip Livingston, Francis Lewis, Lewis Morris
New Jersey: Richard Stockton, John Witherspoon, Francis Hopkinson, John Hart, Abraham Clark
Pennsylvania: Robert Morris, Benjamin Rush, Benjamin Franklin, John Morton, George Clymer, James Smith, George Taylor, James Wilson, George Ross
Delaware: Caesar Rodney, George Read, Thomas McKean
Maryland: Samuel Chase, William Paca, Thomas Stone, Charles Carroll of Carrollton
Virginia: George Wythe, Richard Henry Lee, Thomas Jefferson, Benjamin Harrison, Thomas Nelson, Jr., Francis Lightfoot Lee, Carter Braxton
North Carolina: William Hooper, Joseph Hewes, John Penn
South Carolina: Edward Rutledge, Thomas Heyward, Jr., Thomas Lynch, Jr., Arthur Middleton
Georgia: Button Gwinnett, Lyman Hall, George Walton.

— Appendix 2 —

THE CONSTITUTION OF THE UNITED STATES

We the people of the United States, in order to form a more perfect union, establish justice, insure domestic tranquility, provide for the common defense, promote the general welfare, and secure the blessings of liberty to ourselves and our posterity, do ordain and establish this Constitution for the United States of America.

Article I

Section 1. All legislative powers herein granted shall be vested in a Congress of the United States, which shall consist of a Senate and House of Representatives.

Section 2. The House of Representatives shall be composed of members chosen every second year by the people of the several states, and the electors in each state shall have the qualifications requisite for electors of the most numerous branch of the state legislature.

No person shall be a Representative who shall not have attained to the age of twenty five years, and been seven years a citizen of the United States, and who shall not, when elected, be an inhabitant of that state in which he shall be chosen.

Representatives and direct taxes shall be apportioned among the several states which may be included within this union, according to their respective numbers, which shall be determined by adding to the whole number of free persons, including those bound to service for a term of years, and excluding Indians not taxed, three fifths of all other Persons. The actual Enumeration shall be made within three years after the first meeting of the Congress of the United States, and within every subsequent term of ten years, in such manner as they shall by law direct. The number of Representatives shall not exceed one for every thirty thousand, but each state shall have at least one Representative; and until such enumeration shall be made, the state of New Hampshire shall be entitled to chuse three, Massachusetts eight, Rhode Island and Providence Plantations one, Connecticut five, New York six, New Jersey four, Pennsylvania eight, Delaware one, Maryland six, Virginia ten, North Carolina five, South Carolina five, and Georgia three.

When vacancies happen in the Representation from any state, the executive authority thereof shall issue writs of election to fill such vacancies.

The House of Representatives shall choose their speaker and other officers; and shall have the sole power of impeachment.

Section 3. The Senate of the United States shall be composed of two Senators from each state, chosen by the legislature thereof, for six years; and each Senator shall have one vote.

Immediately after they shall be assembled in consequence of the first election, they shall be divided as equally as may be into three classes. The seats of the Senators of the first class shall be vacated at the expiration of the second year, of the second class at the expiration of the fourth year, and the third class at the expiration of the sixth year, so that one third may be chosen every second year; and if vacancies happen by resignation, or otherwise, during the recess of the legislature of any state, the executive thereof may make temporary appointments until the next meeting of the legislature, which shall then fill such vacancies.

No person shall be a Senator who shall not have attained to the age of thirty years, and been nine years a citizen of the United States and who shall not, when elected, be an inhabitant of that state for which he shall be chosen.

The Vice President of the United States shall be President of the Senate, but shall have no vote, unless they be equally divided.

The Senate shall choose their other officers, and also a President pro tempore, in the absence of the Vice President, or when he shall exercise the office of President of the United States.

The Senate shall have the sole power to try all impeachments. When sitting for that purpose, they shall be on oath or affirmation. When the President of the United States is tried, the Chief Justice shall preside: And no person shall be convicted without the concurrence of two thirds of the members present.

Judgment in cases of impeachment shall not extend further than to removal from office, and disqualification to hold and enjoy any office of honor, trust or profit under the United States: but the party convicted shall nevertheless be liable and subject to indictment, trial, judgment and punishment, according to law.

Section 4. The times, places and manner of holding elections for Senators and Representatives, shall be prescribed in each state by the legislature thereof; but the Congress may at any time by law make or alter such regulations, except as to the places of choosing Senators.

The Congress shall assemble at least once in every year, and such meeting shall be on the first Monday in December, unless they shall by law appoint a different day.

Section 5. Each House shall be the judge of the elections, returns and qualifications of its own members, and a majority of each shall constitute a quorum to do business; but a smaller number may adjourn from day to day, and may be authorized to compel the attendance of absent members, in such manner, and under such penalties as each House may provide.

Each House may determine the rules of its proceedings, punish its members for disorderly behavior, and, with the concurrence of two thirds, expel a member.

Each House shall keep a journal of its proceedings, and from time to time publish the same, excepting such parts as may in their judgment require secrecy; and the yeas and nays of the members of either House on any question shall, at the desire of one fifth of those present, be entered on the journal.

Neither House, during the session of Congress, shall, without the consent of the other, adjourn for more than three days, nor to any other place than that in which the two Houses shall be sitting.

Section 6. The Senators and Representatives shall receive a compensation for their services, to be ascertained by law, and paid out of the treasury of the United States. They shall in all cases, except treason, felony and breach of the peace, be privileged from arrest during their attendance at the session of their respective Houses, and in going to and returning from the same; and for any speech or debate in either House, they shall not be questioned in any other place.

No Senator or Representative shall, during the time for which he was elected, be appointed to any civil office under the authority of the United States, which shall have been created, or the emoluments whereof shall have been increased during such time: and no person holding any office under the United States, shall be a member of either House during his continuance in office.

Section 7. All bills for raising revenue shall originate in the House of Representatives; but the Senate may propose or concur with amendments as on other Bills.

Every bill which shall have passed the House of Representatives and the Senate, shall, before it become a law, be presented to the President of the United States; if he approve he shall sign it, but if not he shall return it, with his objections to that House in which it shall have originated, who shall enter the objections at large on their journal, and proceed to reconsider it. If after such reconsideration two thirds of that House shall agree to pass the bill, it shall be sent, together with the objections, to the other House, by which it shall likewise be reconsidered, and if approved by two thirds of that House, it shall become a law. But in all such cases the votes of both Houses shall be determined by yeas and nays, and the names of the persons voting for and against the bill shall be entered on the journal of each House respectively. If any bill shall not be returned by the President within ten days (Sundays excepted) after it shall have been presented to him, the same shall be a law, in like manner as if he had signed it, unless the Congress by their adjournment prevent its return, in which case it shall not be a law.

Every order, resolution, or vote to which the concurrence of the Senate and House of Representatives may be necessary (except on a question of adjournment) shall be presented to the President of the United States; and before the same shall take effect, shall be approved by him, or being disapproved by him, shall be repassed by two thirds of the Senate and House of Representatives, according to the rules and limitations prescribed in the case of a bill.

Section 8. The Congress shall have power to lay and collect taxes, duties, imposts and excises, to pay the debts and provide for the common defense and general welfare of the United States; but all duties, imposts and excises shall be uniform throughout the United States;

To borrow money on the credit of the United States;

To regulate commerce with foreign nations, and among the several states, and with the Indian tribes;

To establish a uniform rule of naturalization, and uniform laws on the subject of bankruptcies throughout the United States;

To coin money, regulate the value thereof, and of foreign coin, and fix the standard of weights and measures;

To provide for the punishment of counterfeiting the securities and current coin of the United States;

To establish post offices and post roads;

To promote the progress of science and useful arts, by securing for limited times to authors and inventors the exclusive right to their respective writings and discoveries;

To constitute tribunals inferior to the Supreme Court;

To define and punish piracies and felonies committed on the high seas, and offenses against the law of nations;

To declare war, grant letters of marque and reprisal, and make rules concerning captures on land and water;

To raise and support armies, but no appropriation of money to that use shall be for a longer term than two years;

To provide and maintain a navy;

To make rules for the government and regulation of the land and naval forces;

To provide for calling forth the militia to execute the laws of the union, suppress insurrections and repel invasions;

To provide for organizing, arming, and disciplining, the militia, and for governing such part of them as may be employed in the service of the United States, reserving to the states respectively, the appointment of the officers, and the authority of training the militia according to the discipline prescribed by Congress;

To exercise exclusive legislation in all cases whatsoever, over such District (not exceeding ten miles square) as may, by cession of particular states, and the acceptance of Congress, become the seat of the government of the United States, and to exercise like authority over all places purchased by the consent of the legislature of the state in which the same shall be, for the erection of forts, magazines, arsenals, dockyards, and other needful buildings;--And

To make all laws which shall be necessary and proper for carrying into execution the foregoing powers, and all other powers vested by this Constitution in the government of the United States, or in any department or officer thereof.

Section 9. The migration or importation of such persons as any of the states now existing shall think proper to admit, shall not be prohibited by the Congress prior to the year one thousand eight hundred and eight, but a tax or duty may be imposed on such importation, not exceeding ten dollars for each person.

The privilege of the writ of habeas corpus shall not be suspended, unless when in cases of rebellion or invasion the public safety may require it.

No bill of attainder or ex post facto Law shall be passed.

No capitation, or other direct, tax shall be laid, unless in proportion to the census or enumeration herein before directed to be taken.

No tax or duty shall be laid on articles exported from any state.

No preference shall be given by any regulation of commerce or revenue to the ports of one state over those of another: nor shall vessels bound to, or from, one state, be obliged to enter, clear or pay duties in another.

No money shall be drawn from the treasury, but in consequence of appropriations made by law; and a regular statement and account of receipts and expenditures of all public money shall be published from time to time.

No title of nobility shall be granted by the United States: and no person holding any office of profit or trust under them, shall, without the consent of the Congress, accept of any present, emolument, office, or title, of any kind whatever, from any king, prince, or foreign state.

Section 10. No state shall enter into any treaty, alliance, or confederation; grant letters of marque and reprisal; coin money; emit bills of credit; make anything but gold and silver coin a tender in payment of debts; pass any bill of attainder, ex post facto law, or law impairing the obligation of contracts, or grant any title of nobility.

No state shall, without the consent of the Congress, lay any imposts or duties on imports or exports, except what may be absolutely necessary for executing its inspection laws: and the net produce of all duties and imposts, laid by any state on imports or exports, shall be for the use of the treasury of the United States; and all such laws shall be subject to the revision and control of the Congress.

No state shall, without the consent of Congress, lay any duty of tonnage, keep troops, or ships of war in time of peace, enter into any agreement or compact with another state, or with a foreign power, or engage in war, unless actually invaded, or in such imminent danger as will not admit of delay.

Article II

Section 1. The executive power shall be vested in a President of the United States of America. He shall hold his office during the term of four years, and, together with the Vice President, chosen for the same term, be elected, as follows:

Each state shall appoint, in such manner as the Legislature thereof may direct, a number of electors, equal to the whole number of Senators and Representatives to which the State may be entitled in the Congress: but no Senator or Representative, or person holding an office of trust or profit under the United States, shall be appointed an elector.

The electors shall meet in their respective states, and vote by ballot for two persons, of whom one at least shall not be an inhabitant of the same state with themselves. And they shall make a list of all the persons voted for, and of the number of votes for each; which list they shall sign and certify, and transmit sealed to the seat of the government of the United States, directed to the President of the Senate. The President of the Senate shall, in the presence of the Senate and House of Representatives, open all the certificates, and the votes shall then be counted. The person having the greatest number of votes shall be the President, if such number be a majority of the whole number of electors appointed; and if there be more than one who have such majority, and have an equal number of votes, then the House of Representatives shall immediately choose by ballot one of them for President; and if no person have a majority, then from the five highest on the list the said House shall in like manner choose the President. But in choosing the President, the votes shall be taken by States, the representation from each state having one vote; A quorum for this purpose shall consist of a member or members from two thirds of the states, and a majority of all the states shall be necessary to a choice. In every case, after the choice of the President, the person having the greatest number of votes of the electors shall be the Vice President. But if there should remain two or more who have equal votes, the Senate shall choose from them by ballot the Vice President.

The Congress may determine the time of choosing the electors, and the day on which they shall give their votes; which day shall be the same throughout the United States.

No person except a natural born citizen, or a citizen of the United States, at the time of the adoption of this Constitution, shall be eligible to the office of President; neither shall any person be eligible to that office who shall not have attained to the age of thirty five years, and been fourteen Years a resident within the United States.

In case of the removal of the President from office, or of his death, resignation, or inability to discharge the powers and duties of the said office, the same shall devolve on the Vice President, and the Congress may by law provide for the case of removal, death, resignation or inability, both of the President and Vice President, declaring what officer shall then act as President, and such officer shall act accordingly, until the disability be removed, or a President shall be elected.

The President shall, at stated times, receive for his services, a compensation, which shall neither be increased nor diminished during the period for which he shall have been elected, and he shall not receive within that period any other emolument from the United States, or any of them.

Before he enter on the execution of his office, he shall take the following oath or affirmation:--"I do solemnly swear (or affirm) that I will faithfully execute the office of President of the United States, and will to the best of my ability, preserve, protect and defend the Constitution of the United States."

Section 2. The President shall be commander in chief of the Army and Navy of the United States, and of the militia of the several states, when called into the actual service of the United States; he may require the opinion, in writing, of the principal officer in each of the executive departments, upon any subject relating to the duties of their respective offices, and he shall have power to grant reprieves and pardons for offenses against the United States, except in cases of impeachment.

He shall have power, by and with the advice and consent of the Senate, to make treaties, provided two thirds of the Senators present concur; and he shall nominate, and by and with the advice and consent of the Senate, shall appoint ambassadors, other public ministers and consuls, judges of the Supreme Court, and all other officers of the United States, whose appointments are not herein otherwise provided for, and which shall be established by law: but the Congress may by law vest the appointment of such inferior officers, as they think proper, in the President alone, in the courts of law, or in the heads of departments.

The President shall have power to fill up all vacancies that may happen during the recess of the Senate, by granting commissions which shall expire at the end of their next session.

Section 3. He shall from time to time give to the Congress information of the state of the union, and recommend to their consideration such measures as he shall judge necessary and expedient; he may, on extraordinary occasions, convene both Houses, or either of them, and in case of disagreement between them, with respect to the time of adjournment, he may adjourn them to such time as he shall think proper; he shall receive ambassadors and other public ministers; he shall take care that the laws be faithfully executed, and shall commission all the officers of the United States.

Section 4. The President, Vice President and all civil officers of the United States, shall be removed from office on impeachment for, and conviction of, treason, bribery, or other high crimes and misdemeanors.

Article III

Section 1. The judicial power of the United States, shall be vested in one Supreme Court, and in such inferior courts as the Congress may from time to time ordain and establish. The judges, both of the supreme and inferior courts, shall hold their offices during good behaviour, and shall, at stated times, receive for their services, a compensation, which shall not be diminished during their continuance in office.

Section 2. The judicial power shall extend to all cases, in law and equity, arising under this Constitution, the laws of the United States, and treaties made, or which shall be made, under their authority;--to all cases affecting ambassadors, other public ministers and consuls;--to all cases of admiralty and maritime jurisdiction;--to controversies to which the United States shall be a party;--to controversies between two or more states;--between a state and citizens of another state;--between citizens of different states;--between citizens of the same state claiming lands under grants of different states, and between a state, or the citizens thereof, and foreign states, citizens or subjects.

In all cases affecting ambassadors, other public ministers and consuls, and those in which a state shall be party, the Supreme Court shall have original jurisdiction. In all the other cases before mentioned, the Supreme Court shall have appellate jurisdiction, both as to law and fact, with such exceptions, and under such regulations as the Congress shall make.

The trial of all crimes, except in cases of impeachment, shall

be by jury; and such trial shall be held in the state where the said crimes shall have been committed; but when not committed within any state, the trial shall be at such place or places as the Congress may by law have directed.

Section 3. Treason against the United States, shall consist only in levying war against them, or in adhering to their enemies, giving them aid and comfort. No person shall be convicted of treason unless on the testimony of two witnesses to the same overt act, or on confession in open court.

The Congress shall have power to declare the punishment of treason, but no attainder of treason shall work corruption of blood, or forfeiture except during the life of the person attainted.

Article IV

Section 1. Full faith and credit shall be given in each state to the public acts, records, and judicial proceedings of every other state. And the Congress may by general laws prescribe the manner in which such acts, records, and proceedings shall be proved, and the effect thereof.

Section 2. The citizens of each state shall be entitled to all privileges and immunities of citizens in the several states.

A person charged in any state with treason, felony, or other crime, who shall flee from justice, and be found in another state, shall on demand of the executive authority of the state from which he fled, be delivered up, to be removed to the state having jurisdiction of the crime.

No person held to service or labor in one state, under the laws thereof, escaping into another, shall, in consequence of any law or regulation therein, be discharged from such service or labor, but shall be delivered up on claim of the party to whom such service or labor may be due.

Section 3. New states may be admitted by the Congress into this union; but no new states shall be formed or erected within the jurisdiction of any other state; nor any state be formed by the junction of two or more states, or parts of states, without the consent of the legislatures of the states concerned as well as of the Congress.

The Congress shall have power to dispose of and make all needful rules and regulations respecting the territory or other property belonging to the United States; and nothing in this Constitution shall be so construed as to prejudice any claims of the United States, or of any particular state.

Section 4. The United States shall guarantee to every state in this union a republican form of government, and shall protect each of them against invasion; and on application of the legislature, or of the executive (when the legislature cannot be convened) against domestic violence.

Article V

The Congress, whenever two thirds of both houses shall deem it necessary, shall propose amendments to this Constitution, or, on the application of the legislatures of two thirds of the several states, shall call a convention for proposing amendments, which, in either case, shall be valid to all intents and purposes, as part of this Constitution, when ratified by the legislatures of three fourths of the several states, or by conventions in three fourths thereof, as the one or the other mode of ratification may be proposed by the Congress; provided that no amendment which may be made prior to the year one thousand eight hundred and eight shall in any manner affect the first and fourth clauses in the ninth section of the first article; and that no state, without its consent, shall be deprived of its equal suffrage in the Senate.

Article VI

All debts contracted and engagements entered into, before the adoption of this Constitution, shall be as valid against the United States under this Constitution, as under the Confederation.

This Constitution, and the laws of the United States which shall be made in pursuance thereof; and all treaties made, or which shall be made, under the authority of the United States, shall be the supreme law of the land; and the judges in every state shall be bound thereby, anything in the Constitution or laws of any State to the contrary notwithstanding.

The Senators and Representatives before mentioned, and the members of the several state legislatures, and all executive and judicial officers, both of the United States and of the several states, shall be bound by oath or affirmation, to support this Constitution; but no religious test shall ever be required as a qualification to any office or public trust under the United States.

Article VII

The ratification of the conventions of nine states, shall be sufficient for the establishment of this Constitution between the states so ratifying the same.

Done in convention by the unanimous consent of the states present the seventeenth day of September in the year of our Lord one thousand seven hundred and eighty seven and of the independence of the United States of America the twelfth. In witness whereof We have hereunto subscribed our Names,

G. Washington-Presidt. and deputy from Virginia

New Hampshire: John Langdon, Nicholas Gilman

Massachusetts: Nathaniel Gorham, Rufus King

Connecticut: Wm: Saml. Johnson, Roger Sherman

New York: Alexander Hamilton

New Jersey: Wil: Livingston, David Brearly, Wm. Paterson, Jona: Dayton

Pennsylvania: B. Franklin, Thomas Mifflin, Robt. Morris, Geo. Clymer, Thos. FitzSimons, Jared Ingersoll, James Wilson, Gouv Morris

Delaware: Geo: Read, Gunning Bedford jun, John Dickinson, Richard Bassett, Jaco: Broom

Maryland: James McHenry, Dan of St Thos. Jenifer, Danl Carroll

Virginia: John Blair--, James Madison Jr.

North Carolina: Wm. Blount, Richd. Dobbs Spaight, Hu Williamson

South Carolina: J. Rutledge, Charles Cotesworth Pinckney, Charles Pinckney, Pierce Butler

Georgia: William Few, Abr Baldwin

THE BILL OF RIGHTS

Amendments 1-10 of the Constitution

The Conventions of a number of the States having, at the time of adopting the Constitution, expressed a desire, in order to prevent misconstruction or abuse of its powers, that further declaratory and restrictive clauses should be added, and as extending the ground of public confidence in the Government will best insure the beneficent ends of its institution;

Resolved, by the Senate and House of Representatives of the United States of America, in Congress assembled, two-thirds of both Houses concurring, that the following articles be proposed to the Legislatures of the several States, as amendments to the Constitution of the United States; all or any of which articles, when ratified by three-fourths of the said Legislatures, to be valid to all intents and purposes as part of the said Constitution, namely:

Amendment I

Congress shall make no law respecting an establishment of religion, or prohibiting the free exercise thereof; or abridging the freedom of speech, or of the press; or the right of the people peaceably to assemble, and to petition the government for a redress of grievances.

Amendment II

A well regulated militia, being necessary to the security of a free state, the right of the people to keep and bear arms, shall not be infringed.

Amendment III

No soldier shall, in time of peace be quartered in any house, without the consent of the owner, nor in time of war, but in a manner to be prescribed by law.

Amendment IV

The right of the people to be secure in their persons, houses, papers, and effects, against unreasonable searches and seizures, shall not be violated, and no warrants shall issue, but upon probable cause, supported by oath or affirmation, and particularly describing the place to be searched, and the persons or things to be seized.

Amendment V

No person shall be held to answer for a capital, or otherwise infamous crime, unless on a presentment or indictment of a grand jury, except in cases arising in the land or naval forces, or in the militia, when in actual service in time of war or public danger; nor shall any person be subject for the same offense to be twice put in jeopardy of life or limb; nor shall be compelled in any criminal case to be a witness against himself, nor be deprived of life, liberty, or property, without due process of law; nor shall private property be taken for public use, without just compensation.

Amendment VI

In all criminal prosecutions, the accused shall enjoy the right to a speedy and public trial, by an impartial jury of the state and district wherein the crime shall have been committed, which district shall have been previously ascertained by law, and to be informed of the nature and cause of the accusation; to be confronted with the witnesses against him; to have compulsory process for obtaining witnesses in his favor, and to have the assistance of counsel for his defense.

Amendment VII

In suits at common law, where the value in controversy shall exceed twenty dollars, the right of trial by jury shall be preserved, and no fact tried by a jury, shall be otherwise reexamined in any court of the United States, than according to the rules of the common law.

Amendment VIII

Excessive bail shall not be required, nor excessive fines imposed, nor cruel and unusual punishments inflicted.

Amendment IX

The enumeration in the Constitution, of certain rights, shall not be construed to deny or disparage others retained by the people.

Amendment X

The powers not delegated to the United States by the Constitution, nor prohibited by it to the states, are reserved to the states respectively, or to the people.

— *Appendix 4* —

THE BARMEN DECLARATION

In view of the errors of the "German Christians" and of the present Reich Church Administration, which are ravaging the Church and at the same time also shattering the unity of the German Evangelical Church, we confess the following evangelical truths:

1. "I am the Way and the Truth and the Life; no one comes to the Father except through me." John 14:6

"Very truly, I tell you, anyone who does not enter the sheepfold through the gate but climbs in by another way is a thief and a bandit. I am the gate. Whoever enters by me will be saved." John 10:1,9

Jesus Christ, as he is attested to us in Holy Scripture, is the one Word of God whom we have to hear, and whom we have to trust and obey in life and in death.

We reject the false doctrine that the Church could and should recognize as a source of its proclamation, beyond and besides this one Word of God, yet other events, powers, historic figures and truths as God's revelation.

2. "Jesus Christ has been made wisdom and righteousness and sanctification and redemption for us by God." 1 Cor. 1:30

As Jesus Christ is God's comforting pronouncement of the forgiveness of all our sins, so, with equal seriousness, he is also God's vigorous announcement of his claim upon our whole life. Through him there comes to us joyful liberation from the godless ties of this world for free, grateful service to his creatures.

We reject the false doctrine that there could be areas of our life in which we would not belong to Jesus Christ but to other lords, areas in which we would not need justification and sanctification through him.

3. "Let us, however, speak the truth in love, and in every respect grow into him who is the head, into Christ, from whom the whole body is joined together." Eph. 4:15-16

The Christian Church is the community of brethren in which, in Word and Sacrament, through the Holy Spirit, Jesus Christ acts in the present as Lord. With both its faith and its obedience, with both its message and its order, it has to testify in the midst of the sinful world, as the Church of pardoned sinners, that it belongs to him alone and lives and may live by his comfort and under his direction alone, in expectation of his appearing.

We reject the false doctrine that the Church could have permission to hand over the form of its message and of its order to whatever it itself might wish or to the vicissitudes of the prevailing ideological and political convictions of the day.

4. "You know that the rulers of the Gentiles lord it over them, and their great ones are tyrants over them. It will not be so among you; but whoever wishes to have authority over you must be your servant." Matt. 20:25-26

The various offices in the Church do not provide a basis for some to exercise authority over others but for the ministry with which the whole community has been entrusted and charged to be carried out.

We reject the false doctrine that, apart from this ministry, the Church could, and could have permission to, give itself or allow itself to be given special leaders vested with ruling authority.

5. "Fear God. Honor the Emperor." 1 Pet. 2:17

Scripture tells us that by divine appointment the State, in this still unredeemed world in which also the Church is situated, has the task of maintaining justice and peace, so far as human discernment and human ability make this possible, by means of the threat and use of force. The Church acknowledges with gratitude and reverence toward God the benefit of this, his appointment. It draws attention to God's Dominion, God's commandment and justice, and with these the responsibility of those who rule and those who are ruled. It trusts and obeys the power of the Word, by which God upholds all things.

We reject the false doctrine that beyond its special commission the State should and could become the sole and total order of human life and so fulfill the vocation of the Church as well.

We reject the false doctrine that beyond its special commission the Church should and could take on the nature, tasks and dignity which belong to the State and thus become itself an organ of the State.

6. "See, I am with you always, to the end of the age." Matt. 28:20
"God's Word is not fettered." 2 Tim. 2:9

The Church's commission, which is the foundation of its freedom, consists in this: in Christ's stead, and so in the service of his own Word and work, to deliver all people, through preaching and sacrament, the message of the free grace of God.

We reject the false doctrine that with human vainglory the Church could place the Word and work of the Lord in the service of self-chosen desires, purposes and plans.

The Confessing Synod of the German Evangelical Church declares that it sees in the acknowledgment of these truths and in the rejection of these errors the indispensable theological basis of the German Evangelical Church as a confederation of Confessing Churches. It calls upon all who can stand in solidarity with its Declaration to be mindful of these theological findings in all their decisions concerning Church and State. It appeals to all concerned to return to unity in faith, hope and love.

Verbum Dei manet in aeternum.

The Word of God will last for ever.

— *Notes* —

[1] http://quotes.telemanage.ca/quotes.nsf/
QuotesByCat?ReadForm&Start=1&Count=1000&ExpandView&
RestrictToCategory=Society.

[2] http://www.thetexasmercury.com/articles/cantrell/
JC20030303.html.

[3] Prima Lifestyles, 2002. Though DiLorenzo's book is not a historian's effort, it does what virtually no American historian has had the courage to do: challenge all the self-serving myths that America believes about Lincoln. On that score, DiLorenzo is to be commended for standing up to the propaganda barrage that has only become worse since 9/11.

[4] Oxford Press, 2001.

[5] http://www.townhall.com/columnists/calthomas/ct20030722.shtml.

[6] http://www.ecm-inc.com/election2000/stories/september/
21phillips.html.

[7] http://atheism.about.com/b/a/016039.htm.

[8] http://www.womensenews.org/article.cfm/dyn/aid/1028/context/
archive.

[9] http://www.lewrockwell.com/archives/fm/1-99.html.

[10] http://www.lewrockwell.com/orig3/greenhut1.html.

[11] http://www.lewrockwell.com/orig3/d-black1.html.

[12] http://www.lewrockwell.com/yates/yates69.html.

[13] Charles Adams, *When in the Course of Human Events: Arguing the Case for Southern Secession* (Rowman and Littlefield, 2000).

[14] http://www.ndol.org/blueprint/2001_nov-dec/05_just_war.html.

[15] Thomas DiLorenzo, *The Real Lincoln* (Prima Lifestyles, 2002).

[16] http://www.american-partisan.com/cols/2002/antle/qtr2/0624.htm.

[17] http://www.heritage.org/Research/Budget/BG1703.cfm.

[18] http://www.cato.org/new/02-02/02-02-28r.html.

[19] http://www.lewrockwell.com/paul/paul80.html.

[20] Murray Rothbard, *Man, Economy, and State* (Los Angeles: Nash Publishing, 1970) p. 818.

[21] David Hall, *Savior or Servant? Putting Government In Its Place* (Oak Ridge, Tennessee: The Kuyper Institute, 1996) p. 389.

[22] http://www.sepschool.org/.

[23] http://www.ctlibrary.com/ct/1997/oct6/7tb088.html.

[24] http://www.patriotist.com/lgarch/20000410.htm.

[25] http://www.antiwar.com/orig/hunsinger3.html.

[26] http://toogoodreports.com/column/general/baldwin/20030216-fss.htm.

[27] http://politics.guardian.co.uk/foreignaffairs/story/0,11538,903844,00.html.

[28] http://www.whitehouse.gov/news/releases/2003/02/20030226-11.html.

[29] http://www.buchanan.org/pa-95-1128.html.

[30] http://www.cnn.com/2000/ALLPOLITICS/stories/07/30/convention.wrap/.

[31] http://www.declaration.net/news.asp?docID=3624&y=2003.

[32] http://www.lewrockwell.com/paul/paul76.html.

[33] http://www.luther95.org/NELCA/internos/moeller.htm.

[34] Leslie Newbigin, *The Other Side of 1984* (Consul Oecumenique, 1983) pp. 36-37.

Printed in the United States
24424LVS00001B/268

9 781413 730197